Library of
Davidson College

Income, employment, and urban residential location

**Institute for Research on Poverty
Monograph Series**

Vernon L. Allen, Editor, *Psychological Factors in Poverty*

Frederick Williams, Editor, *Language and Poverty: Perspectives on a Theme*

Murray Edelman, *Politics as Symbolic Action: Mass Arousal and Quiescence*

Joel F. Handler and Ellen Jane Hollingsworth, *"The Deserving Poor": A Study of Welfare Administration*

Robert J. Lampman, *Ends and Means of Reducing Income Poverty*

Larry L. Orr, Robinson G. Hollister, and Myron J. Lefcowitz, Editors, with the assistance of Karen Hester, *Income Maintenance: Interdisciplinary Approaches to Research*

Charles E. Metcalf, *An Econometric Model of the Income Distribution*

Glen G. Cain and Harold W. Watts, Editors, *Income Maintenance and Labor Supply: Econometric Studies*

Joel F. Handler, *The Coercive Social Worker: British Lessons for American Social Services*

Larry L. Orr, *Income, Employment, and Urban Residential Location*

In Preparation

Irene Lurie, *Integrating Income Maintenance Programs*

Stanley H. Masters, *Black–White Income Differentials: Empirical Studies and Policy Implications*

Income, employment, and urban residential location

Larry L. Orr
Department of Health, Education, and Welfare
Washington, D. C.

ACADEMIC PRESS   New York San Francisco London
A Subsidiary of Harcourt Brace Jovanovich, Publishers

This book is one of a series sponsored by the Institute for
Research on Poverty of the University of Wisconsin pursuant to
the provisions of the Economic Opportunity Act of 1964.

Copyright © 1975 by the Regents of the University of Wisconsin
System on behalf of the Institute for Research on Poverty.
All rights reserved.
No part of this publication may be reproduced or transmitted
in any form or by any means, electronic or mechanical, including
photocopy, recording, or any information storage and retrieval
system, without permission in writing from the publisher.

Academic Press, Inc.
111 Fifth Avenue, New York, New York 10003

United Kingdom Edition published by
Academic Press, Inc. (London) Ltd.
24/28 Oval Road, London NW1

Library of Congress Cataloging in Publication Data

Orr, Larry L
    Income, employment, and urban residential location.

    (Monograph series – Institute for Research on Poverty)
    Based on the author's thesis, Massachusetts Institute
of Technology, 1967.
    Bibliography: p.
    Includes index.
    1.   Land subdivision–United States.   2.   Residential
mobility–United States.   3.   Income–United States.
4.   Labor supply–United States.   5.   Municipal government–Unites States.   I.   Title.   II.   Series: Wisconsin. University–Madison. Institute for Research on
Poverty. Monograph series.
HD259.07 1975   301.36   74-17966
ISBN 0–12–528440–3

Printed in the United States of America

To Bette

Institute for Research on Poverty

The Institute for Research on Poverty is a national center for research established at the University of Wisconsin in 1966 by a grant from the Office of Economic Opportunity. Its primary objective is to foster basic, multidisciplinary research into the nature and causes of poverty and means to combat it.

In addition to increasing the basic knowledge from which policies aimed at the elimination of poverty can be shaped, the Institute strives to carry analysis beyond the formulation and testing of fundamental generalizations to the development and assessment of relevant policy alternatives.

The Institute endeavors to bring together scholars of the highest caliber whose primary research efforts are focused on the problem of poverty, the distribution of income, and the analysis and evaluation of social policy, offering staff members wide opportunity for interchange of ideas, maximum freedom for research into basic questions about poverty and social policy, and dissemination of their findings.

Contents

Foreword   xi
Preface   xiii

1   The problem, an approach, and a perspective

    I. Introduction   1
    II. The method of analysis   6
    III. Relation to previous studies   8

2   The theoretical model

    I. Quantification of activity levels   15
    II. Assumptions of the model   18
    III. The determinants of net density in a free market   22
    IV. The determinants of areal shares in a free market   31

	V. The effect of density zoning on gross density	35
	VI. The market value of land	39

3 Variables of the model

    I. Land use categories   41
    II. Site costs   43
    III. Quality characteristics   44
    IV. Minimum zoned lot size   53
    V. Property taxes   54

4 Empirical tests of the model

    I. The nature of the sample and estimation technique   59
    II. Preliminary tests of the model   64
    III. Estimation of land use gross densities: residential land uses   70
    IV. Estimation of land use gross densities: employment uses   89

5 Summary of findings and implications for policy

    I. The empirical findings   103
    II. Implications for public policy   108

Appendix Sources of data for cities and towns   121
Bibliography   125
Index   131

Foreword

The structure and function of the urban metropolis have an important impact on the well-being of its inhabitants. The urban poor, in particular, are affected by the market and other forces that operate within the urban economy to determine residential housing and employment patterns, crime, congestion, and pollution levels, and the quantity and quality of public services. Because relief from the more undesirable characteristics of urban life can be obtained if one has the means, the urban poor—who form more than one-third of the nation's poor—are particularly vulnerable to the complex set of social conditions that have come to be known as "the urban problem."

In this monograph, Larry L. Orr presents a theoretical and empirical analysis of the complex set of interacting variables that form the urban environment. Although his study is based on a simple characterization of the urban economy, it is a significant step toward an integrated analysis of the numerous interrelated forces that determine where both poor and nonpoor live and work in the city and the quality of their lives in both areas. As such, it represents a significant advance over a good deal of earlier work focusing on individual problem sectors, such as the urban labor market, urban transportation, and urban housing.

Dr. Orr's analysis focuses on a number of questions that are central to the development of effective urban and antipoverty policy. In choosing where to live in the city, how dependent are poor households on the location of jobs and the costs of housing, relative to higher-income families? Do restrictive density-zoning ordinances in the suburbs operate to keep poor families concentrated in the central city? Have employment opportunities in the central city decreased because of the high property tax costs in these areas due to the flight of higher-income families to the suburbs? Through application of the tools of location theory and local public finance economics, empirical results are obtained that contribute to answering these questions. These results shed light on the relative effectiveness of a wide range of antipoverty and urban development policies —local taxation and public service policies, federal revenue sharing, public housing, rent supplements, urban transportation, and income maintenance legislation. In the final chapter of the monograph, Dr. Orr draws some of the implications of his study for policy alternatives in all of these areas.

During part of the time this book was being prepared, Dr. Orr was a member of the economics faculty at the University of Wisconsin—Madison and of the staff of the Institute for Research on Poverty. Currently, he is Director of Income Security Policy Research in the Office of the Assistant Secretary for Planning and Evaluation of the Department of Health, Education, and Welfare.

Robert H. Haveman
Director, Institute for Research on Poverty

Preface

Much of the research incorporated in this monograph was initially undertaken in the course of my dissertation, which was submitted to the Massachusetts Institute of Technology in 1967. Further work was completed while I was a member of the research staffs of the Institute for Research on Poverty at the University of Wisconsin and of the U. S. Office of Economic Opportunity. I want to gratefully acknowledge the advice and assistance of a number of people at these and other institutions.

Daniel M. Holland first aroused my interest in issues of local public finance, and has maintained a continuing interest in my work in this area. He, along with Edwin Kuh and E. Cary Brown, provided valuable advice, encouragement, and guidance as members of my dissertation committee. Others who provided helpful suggestions and assistance at various stages of the research include Ira Lowry, Jerome Rothenberg, David Black, Eugene Smolensky, and Larry Thompson.

A number of individuals in private and public organizations provided indispensable assistance in the difficult task of data collection; without their help this study would not have been possible. Most of these individuals are noted in the Appendix. I want particularly to thank William Presson of the M.I.T. library staff.

Financial support for the early stages of this research was provided by grants from the National Science Foundation and the Committee on Urban Economics of Resources for the Future, Inc. Later work was supported in part by funds granted to the Institute for Research on Poverty by the Office of Economic Opportunity, pursuant to the Economic Opportunity Act of 1964.

Marjean Jondrow, of the Institute for Research on Poverty, and Karla O'Brien, of the Harvard–M.I.T. Joint Center for Urban Studies, provided valuable editorial assistance in the preparation of the manuscript.

The opinions and conclusions expressed in this monograph are those of the author and do not represent the views or policy of any of the above-mentioned organizations.

Finally, I am indebted to my friends and colleagues Robert Haveman and Robinson Hollister for encouraging me to revise and extend this study for publication.

Income,
employment, and
urban residential
location

1

The problem, an approach, and a perspective

I. Introduction

Among the most prominent and seemingly intractable problems of American society are those that arise from, or achieve their most acute forms within, the urban environment. The catalogue of "urban problems" is by now familiar: unemployment, crime, racial segregation, inadequate and unsafe housing, high taxes and deteriorating services, suburban sprawl and urban congestion, to name but a few. The long list of programs designed to eliminate or ameliorate these conditions is equally familiar: job training and public employment, public housing, urban renewal, community action, and highway construction and rapid transit are among the many. It is generally agreed, however, that these efforts either have not had substantial impact upon the social conditions they address or have created unintended side effects that may be worse than the problems they solve. This disturbing situation is matched by another: Little seems to be known about how to design programs with greater promise of success.

In large part, the reason for our inability to cope effectively with urban problems lies in the complexity of the urban environment itself. The natural inclination of program designers and social scientists alike to focus on individual problem areas —such as housing, education, and transportation—runs afoul of the highly interdependent nature of the urban environment. Any substantial impact on any one narrowly defined urban subsystem will have repercussions in other subsystems, repercussions that often run counter to the objectives of the initial intervention. It is essential to understand and quantify these interdependent relationships if public policy is to address urban problems effectively. Unfortunately, the current state of knowledge of the urban structure is meager at best. Hypotheses and theories abound, but few of these have been empirically tested, and many have not even been stated with sufficient precision to allow empirical testing.

Sound empirical understanding of urban social and economic systems is especially important for public policy relating to the poverty population. About 33 percent of all poor American families live in the central cities where urban problems are most acute, and that percentage has been steadily rising over the last decade.[1] Moreover, society's ability—or inability—to deal effectively with urban problems is likely to have a disproportionate effect on the lives of the poor; the poor have the least ability to shape or choose the environment in which they live and the least resources to adjust to the changes that are constantly occurring in that environment.

---

[1] U. S. Bureau of the Census, *Current Population Reports*, Series P-60, No. 81, "Characteristics of Low-Income Population, 1970" (Washington, D. C.: U. S. Government Printing Office): 5.

I. Introduction

This study is not, however, another essay on the plight of the urban poor. Rather, it is an attempt to further our understanding of the interrelated social and economic forces that shape the urban environment and that determine where the poor—and the nonpoor—will live, the job opportunities that will be available to them, the housing they will occupy, and the rents they will pay. Only when we have achieved an adequate understanding of the underlying structure of the urban environment can we hope to design programs that can deal effectively with its problems.

A summary description of those forces that would be generally accepted by students of urban problems might run something like the following. Low-income families favor central residential locations because of the proximity of employment opportunities and the availability of low-cost housing. Central-city housing is relatively cheap because it is old and deteriorating and because its high density allows relatively low site rents per dwelling. Families with higher incomes, on the other hand, are more willing to travel longer distances to work in exchange for the more spacious, low-density residential patterns that are feasible only in the suburbs where land is cheaper. This option, however, is often precluded for the poor by racial discrimination and restrictive suburban zoning ordinances designed to preserve the low-density pattern of residential development.

This de facto residential segregation by income class places central-city governments at a disadvantage in financing vital municipal services, such as education, police and fire protection, parks, and recreation. Low-income families typically contribute less to municipal revenues than they consume in municipal services. Low-cost housing is also low-value housing, and the residential base of the property tax—the mainstay of municipal finance—is correspondingly smaller than that of the more affluent suburbs. Historically, the commercial and industrial tax base of the central city has tended to redress this imbalance; but in recent decades an increasing proportion of new industrial and commercial activity has begun to locate in the suburban ring rather than the urban core. These trends have resulted in rapidly rising tax rates and deteriorating public services in the central cities.

The process is, of course, self-reinforcing. High tax rates encourage new commercial and industrial activities to locate in the lower-cost suburbs, further widening the tax base disparity. High-income families move to the suburbs to enjoy the higher quality schools and municipal services available there and to take advantage of the more attractive employment opportunities afforded by new suburban firms.

The poor are left in the central cities and suffer a variety of adverse consequences. The lower quality of municipal services in the central city not only decreases their current welfare but also—especially in the case of education—their chances of escape from poverty in the long run. Similarly, the decentralization of commerce and industry reduces relative employment opportunities in the urban core, further weakening the self-sufficiency of the poor. Even the efforts of central-city governments to alleviate their financial plight often have adverse effects that fall most heavily on the poor. Urban renewal, undertaken to shore up the central-city tax base, uproots families and reduces the stock of low-cost housing. Efforts to keep upper-income residents in the city by improving municipal services are often focused on upper-income sections of the city with a resultant reduction in the financial support and quality of services to the residentially segregated poor. On the tax side, city assessors appear to systematically favor nonresidential and high-income residential properties to placate the more mobile (and powerful) taxpayers.

All of this is, of course, a highly stylized version of urban dynamics. It may be that this overstates the importance of economic forces in general and municipal finance in particular. What seems clear, however, is that residential location by income class, the spatial distribution of employment opportunities, and the provision and financing of municipal services are

I. Introduction

all intimately intertwined in our metropolitan areas. And the outcomes of this interdependent system have important implications for the well-being of the urban poor.

This study is an attempt to shed some light on at least the central features of the urban spatial location process. A model of the spatial distribution of employment and residence by income class in an urban area is developed and estimated in order to test the following major hypotheses:

1. The residential location of low-income households is more sensitive to employment opportunities and housing costs than that of higher-income households.
2. The residential location of high-income families is sensitive to municipal finance variables, such as service quality and tax rates.
3. Restrictive density-zoning ordinances in suburban communities operate to exclude low-income families.
4. The distribution of employment opportunities in a metropolitan area is sensitive to land and tax costs.
5. Property taxes levied on rental housing are shifted forward to tenants.

Each of these hypotheses has important implications for the way in which we view the urban poverty problem in the context of residential location and the policies we devise to cope with it. There are various policy instruments that are capable of affecting the spatial distribution of urban residential and economic activity, depending upon the strength and nature of the relationships hypothesized above. Most obvious are the traditional tools of municipal finance: taxation, service provision, and zoning regulations. But there are also a number of state and national policy instruments that can, directly or indirectly, affect urban locational patterns. Federal and state governments can, through direct assistance to individuals and special-purpose grants or general-purpose transfers to local governments, act to redress the fiscal imbalance between city and suburbs. Housing policies, urban renewal, and transportation programs can augment or ameliorate the trend toward centralization of the low-income population. Open-housing legislation and enforcement can lower the barriers to free choice on the part of minority families. School desegregation and consolidation across political lines, and state or metropolitan tax base equalization can serve to equalize the quality of public services within the urban area.

This study is principally concerned with the impact of *municipal* government policy upon intraurban location, not because that is necessarily the best level of government at which to approach urban problems, but because that is the level at which governmental policy has traditionally been formulated in the American metropolis. Thus, it is the level at which the impact of public policy can be measured empirically. The policy variables with which we shall be concerned are the traditional governmental tools of taxing, spending, and regulation. The basic question to be answered is what effect manipulation of these variables would have upon the socioeconomic composition of the individual community. The analysis presented is thus, in one sense, a marginal analysis; we shall approach the problem from the viewpoint of a single municipal governmental authority, which takes the actions of all other such authorities as beyond its control and attempts to influence the pattern of its own development by exercising those controls at its disposal. Empirical analysis of the effects of governmental policy at this level can, however, give some indication of the direct or indirect effects of policies that might be pursued by other levels of government.

II. The method of analysis

Any attempt to assess empirically the impact of decentralized municipal governmental decisions upon the distribution of urban economic activity requires heroic simplification of the complex economic and spatial relationships that characterize

II. The method of analysis

the modern metropolis. This study is no exception, but every attempt is made to retain at least the most essential features of those relationships.

The analysis proceeds on the assumption that the spatial distribution of households and industry in a particular urban area is the outcome of the workings of the urban land market in allocating space to competing uses. For purposes of both theoretical and empirical analysis, the entire urban area is broken down into numerous subregions, or municipalities, within which sites are assumed to be auctioned off to the highest bidder. The peculiar characteristics of each municipality determine the value of its sites to a land user engaged in a particular activity and, therefore, the price he is willing to bid for a site.

Those land users who value most highly the mix of governmental and other characteristics found in a particular municipality will be successful in obtaining sites there. Thus, the land use pattern, as well as the price of land, is determined, with land price viewed as the equilibrating mechanism in the analysis. The land market provides, then, a direct link between the characteristics of local government and the industrial and residential makeup of the municipality.

In Chapter 2 a theoretical model of the equilibrium land use pattern for any particular municipality will be derived. This is basically a Ricardian land market model, with land rent treated as a residual after payment of the market returns of all other factors of production. Land rents are assumed to vary with the quality of the land in its most productive use. The quality of land depends on the specific characteristics of the municipality, including its local governmental policy variables.

We shall consider eight distinct classes of land use: three categories of industrial and commercial use, and five income classes of residential use. The relative densities of these eight land uses characterize the industrial and residential composition of the community.

The model is general enough to include virtually any

municipal characteristic or governmental policy variable that can be precisely quantified. The community attributes selected for analysis here were chosen as those which seemed most relevant on a priori grounds, within the constraints of available data. The governmental policy variables selected fall into three classes: taxes, services, and zoning regulations. At the local level, the predominant source of tax revenue is the property tax, which in 1962 accounted for 88 percent of all local tax receipts in the United States.[2] Therefore, the equalized property tax rate is used as the sole tax variable. Proxies for a wide variety of local governmental services—education, streets and highways, police and fire protection, sewage disposal and water supply, parks and recreation—are considered explicitly. Finally, a measure of local residential density zoning is introduced. The rationale for the selection of these variables and their quantification is discussed in Chapter 3.

In Chapter 4 empirical estimates are made of the impact of these policy variables, as well as other nongovernmental factors, on the distribution of population and employment, within the context of the theoretical model. The implications of the results for several related questions—for example, the incidence of the local property tax on rental properties—are also discussed. Chapter 5 provides a brief summary of the findings and some policy implications of the study.

III. Relation to previous studies

This study builds on the work of a number of writers in the field of local public finance and urban location theory. Although it is not possible to survey all of the existing literature in these fields, it is useful to briefly indicate the relation of this investigation to previous studies.

---

[2] Dick Netzer, *Economics of the Property Tax* (Washington, D. C.: The Brookings Institution, 1966), p. 9, Table 1–2.

III. Relation to previous studies

Traditionally, local public finance and urban location theory have been treated as distinct fields, with little attempt to integrate the two; one of the primary purposes of this study is to provide such an integration. In neither field has much effort been devoted to assessing the effect of local governmental decisions upon the distribution of urban economic activity.

At first blush, it might appear that there is a wealth of empirical information on at least one aspect of this study—the impact of local taxation on location decisions, particularly in the case of manufacturing plant location.[3] On closer examination, however, one finds that virtually all of the work in this area relates to *interurban* location decisions, that is, location decisions among alternative urban areas, which may even be in different parts of the country, rather than the *intraurban* location decision, which is the focus of this study. The results of these inquiries have been uniformly negative; local tax differentials among urban areas have been found to be a relatively insignificant factor in the location decision.[4]

The relatively minor role played by tax considerations at the interurban level does not, however, preclude a much more substantial effect at the intraurban level. At least one writer has argued rather persuasively that the factors generally cited as dominating the interurban location decision (raw materials sources, markets, labor supply and costs, and power and fuel

---

[3] See, e.g., John F. Due, "Studies of State-Local Tax Influences on Location of Industry," *National Tax Journal* 14(June 1961): 163–173. Wilbur Thompson and John Mattila, *An Econometric Model of Postwar State Industrial Development* (Detroit: Wayne State University Press, 1959); C. C. Bloom, *State and Local Tax Differentials* (Iowa City: Bureau of Business Research, State University of Iowa, 1955); and W. D. Ross, "Tax Concessions and Their Effect," *Proceedings of the National Tax Association*, 1957, pp. 216–224.

[4] Netzer's interpretation of the available evidence is that: "The tentative conclusion offered here is that property tax differentials among states and regions of the country probably have had a relatively limited impact on allocative efficiency overall . . . [*Economics of the Property Tax*, p. 116]."

costs) tend to vary only slightly within any particular urban area.[5] Once a specific urban area has been selected, he contends, other factors, such as land costs and taxes, come into prominence.

Much less empirical work has been done on the importance of local governmental services in location decisions. Several writers have, however, discussed the theoretical aspects of locational effects of local public services provided out of municipal tax revenues. Probably the best-known theoretical treatment is the work of Charles M. Tiebout, which has become a classic in the field of public finance.[6] The "Tiebout hypothesis" contends that households choose among a variety of fixed tax-service "packages" offered by different communities in a region, just as buyers choose among different goods at different prices in a private market. If costs of mobility are ignored, households will "vote with their feet" by selecting the community that best suits their preferences for public goods, thereby automatically segregating themselves according to their tastes for local public services.

Although the Tiebout model is basically similar to the view of local public goods and taxation adopted here, it is a much narrower interpretation of the location process. Tiebout assumes away all differences among communities except those relating directly to local taxes and public services. Thus he excludes consideration of transportation costs and differential proximity to economic activity, considerations that are central to urban location theory. Indeed, his model can be characterized as a location model in which space, per se, plays no essential role.

---

[5] T. E. McMillan, "Determinants of Plant Location," *Land Economics* 41(August 1965): 239.

[6] Charles M. Tiebout, "A Pure Theory of Local Expenditures," *Journal of Political Economy* 64(October 1956): 416–424. A somewhat more general model along these same lines is developed in Bryan Ellickson, "Jurisdictional Fragmentation and Residential Choice," *Proceedings of the American Economic Association*, May 1971, pp. 334–339.

III. Relation to previous studies

Despite its shortcomings, however, the Tiebout model provides a potentially useful description of the interrelation among household preferences, spatial distribution, and local public finance. It demonstrates theoretically the basis for the dependence of residential location decision on municipal public finance characteristics; this dependence can easily be carried over to a more general model in the spirit of modern urban location theory.

The final local policy variable to be considered is the structure of zoning regulations concerned with local residential density. Such regulations are a long-standing feature of local regulations, but only recently has a systematic attempt been made to assess their impact on residential location. The popularly held belief is that low-density maximums (high minimum lot sizes) discourage low-income residence by encouraging more expensive residential development. Probably the best theoretical treatment of the subject is that of Alonso.[7] He concludes that such regulations can, if sufficiently stringent, favor development at a higher income level than would be the case in a free market. He also notes, however, that in suburban communities where this type of zoning is strictest, market forces favor high-income development anyway, so that there is no necessary presumption that the effect is substantial. Such empirical research as has been done on the question tends to cast doubt on the existence of a strong "exclusion effect" operating against low-income households. At least two studies have found that lot size is not strongly correlated with the sale price of homes.[8]

---

[7] William Alonso, *Location and Land Use: Toward a General Theory of Land Rent* (Cambridge, Massachusetts: Harvard University Press, 1964), pp. 117–125.

[8] James G. Coke and Charles S. Liebman, "Political Values and Population Density Control," *Land Economics* 37(1961): 347–361; and Massachusetts Department of Commerce and the Urban and Regional Studies Section, Massachusetts Institute of Technology, *The Effects of Large Lot Size on Residential Development*, Urban Land Institute Technical Bulletin No. 32 (Washington, D. C.: Urban Land Institute, 1958).

As is evident from the foregoing, previous studies of the locational consequences of municipal policy decisions have, with few exceptions, proceeded outside the formal framework of urban location theory.[9] This is perhaps to be expected because only recently have consistent general equilibrium models of urban location been developed.[10] However, these models have been cast at a high level of abstraction, assuming away virtually all intraurban differences other than geographic location, and apparently leaving little room for inclusion of nonspatial dissimilarities among subregions of the urban area. Indeed, even without the complications involved in introducing nonspatial characteristics, empirical estimation of such theoretical models would appear to be a formidable task.[11]

The goal set here is a much less ambitious one; rather than introducing public finance variables into a full-blown urban location model, a model of the urban land market is developed that incorporates most of the essential features of such models and adds local public-policy variables. Rather than attempting

---

[9] As one writer has characterized the existing literature: "Economists, for the most part, have analyzed residential location and local government as if they operated in complete isolation from one another. Most theories of residential location fail to recognize even the existence of local political jurisdictions. Theories of fiscal federalism . . . abstract completely from the question of why households decide to live within a particular jurisdiction [Ellickson, "Jurisdictional Fragmentation and Residential Choice," p. 334]."

[10] See, e.g., Alonso, *Location and Land Use*; Lowden Wingo, Jr., *Transportation and Urban Land* (Washington: Resources for the Future, 1961); Edwin S. Mills, "An Aggregative Model of Resource Allocation in a Metropolitan Area," *Proceedings of the American Economic Association*, May, 1967, pp. 197–210; and Richard F. Muth, *Cities and Housing* (Chicago: University of Chicago Press, 1969).

[11] The most notable exception to this general proposition is the work of Muth, *Cities and Housing*. He provides detailed empirical support for many of the relationships derived from his theoretical model of the urban housing market. Muth does not, however, test the influence of municipal governmental variables upon the spatial variables of his model.

III. Relation to previous studies

to determine the levels of all the relevant variables throughout the entire urban area simultaneously, the analysis focuses upon the determinants of land use allocation at the subregional level. Certain aspects of the overall urban economy, notably relative product prices, incomes, and population, that would be endogenous to a truly general equilibrium model are taken as exogenous here. In general, the emphasis is on the supply side rather than the demand side of product markets in order to focus upon the relationships between land, labor, and capital, that characterize the dispersion of economic activity. Admittedly, these are regrettable simplifications of the theoretically correct general equilibrium model, but these modifications appear to be necessary if the analysis is to be suitable for empirical testing.

The more important concepts of general equilibrium location theory that are to be preserved in the analysis may be briefly summarized. The central feature of most urban location models is the concept of accessibility to economic activity. Households wish to be near employment sites and firms wish to locate near product markets or labor supplies. In the usual abstract theoretical case, where all productive activities and markets are concentrated at a single point, accessibility can be measured simply as distance or transportation cost to the central market. Utility and profit maximization results in market demand prices for land that are a decreasing function of distance from the urban core. As a corollary of this model, if land is a superior good, each land user demands more land at lower market prices, so that land use density also is a decreasing function of distance from the core. Individual households and firms locate at those sites that best suit their preferences for land and accessibility, given the market trade-off between land rents and distance from the market.

In this study the concept of accessibility is generalized to allow for dispersed economic activity by means of a "potential" index. The value of accessibility (and other site characteristics) to each use is weighed against the level of competing bids from all other uses to determine which use will be successful in obtaining the site in competitive bidding. It turns out that, as in the standard location theory model, net density of any particular land use will vary directly with land rents and, ceteris paribus, inversely with accessibility. In contrast to the abstract theoretical location model, however, accessibility appears as only one of a number of site characteristics that influence land rents and the distribution of land uses.

II. Assumptions of the model

Each industry is assumed to use inputs of land, labor, and capital. The prices of labor and capital inputs are assumed to be fixed exogenously and to be uniform over the entire metropolitan area. This is a reasonable assumption if nonland inputs are sufficiently mobile that their rates of return tend to be set by national or regional labor and capital markets. The return to land, on the other hand, is viewed as a residual after payment of returns to nonland factors and is allowed to vary from site to site within the metropolitan area. Finally, the market price of each industry's output is taken to be uniform over the entire metropolitan area. This follows from the assumption of perfect competition in the product market.

For nonresidential industries, we may define output in physical units, and assume a standard neoclassical production function, which allows smooth substitution among factors of production, with diminishing returns to each input. We assume constant returns to scale in each industry, consistent with the existence of perfect competition.

For industries producing housing services, however, the definition of a unit of output presents a difficult problem. There is no single unambiguous physical measure of the quantity of housing represented by a given structure situated on a lot of a particular size and location. Instead, for each industry producing housing services we define a theoretical construct, H, that measures the various different combinations of capital and land in units of equal value to the consumer. The price of a unit of H is by definition, then, a constant over the entire urban area. We assume that the functional relationship between factor inputs and output of H has the same general properties as the neoclassical production functions assumed for nonhousing industries. Strictly speaking, however, this relationship cannot be called a production function since it is not a physical measure but depends upon consumers' tastes. Still, it seems reasonable to assume that production of housing services measured in units of equal value to consumers will obey the same laws of diminishing returns, smooth substitution, and constant returns to scale as those exhibited by a neoclassical production function.

This treatment of the production of housing services should make clear why it is desirable to segment the overall housing market into several different "industries" producing services for households at different income levels. We are implicitly assuming that households of (approximately) equal incomes have the same tastes with regard to substitution between land and nonland factors in housing. Thus, a single production relation will be appropriate for all households within a given income range.[1] Households with markedly different incomes, however, will undoubtedly have significantly different preferences with regard to combinations of land and nonland factors in housing; thus, different production relations are required.

One final theoretical concept is needed to complete the model and to allow mathematical derivation of its equilibrium properties. Since the locational and amenity values of land vary from site to site within the uban area, account must be taken of the peculiar characteristics of individual sites. This may be accomplished by measuring the land input in terms of "effective" acres, which are homogeneous from the standpoint of production, rather than geographic acres, which have varying productivity depending upon local site characteristics. To do this, the land input, T, which is measured in geographic acres, is weighted by a quality index, q, to obtain effective acres, qT.[2] We simply postulate that such an index exists and that it is a

---

[1] Ideally, one should use some measure of "normal" or "permanent" income to segregate households according to housing preferences. Unfortunately, this kind of data was not available for the empirical estimates made in Chapter 4, so current income is used.

[2] The index q bears a close relationship to the index of Harrod-neutral technical change employed in neoclassical growth models to allow for the changing productivity of labor over time. Not surprisingly, many of the formal characteristics of intertemporal production functions with Harrod-neutral technical change will therefore carry over to the present cross-sectional model with varying productivity of land.

II. Assumptions of the model

unique function of quantifiable site characteristics. The site characteristics to be considered in the empirical analysis of Chapter 4 include the accessibility of the site to economic activity and various measures of public services provided to the site. Local property taxes and density zoning regulations, the other two important municipal governmental policy variables included in this study, are not included in the quality index but are considered separately. These variables have been excluded because they do not directly affect the productivity of land in its various uses. Rather, the property tax affects the optimal net density of land use only through its effect upon the cost of non-land factors of production. Density zoning affects both the net density of land use and the allocation of land among uses by restricting the range of uses to which sites may be put; it represents a restriction on the free operation of the land market. These policy variables will, therefore, be considered separately from the other site characteristics included in the quality index.

At no point in the theoretical or empirical analysis will it be necessary to specify the precise form of the functional dependence of q upon these site characteristics. From the definition of q, however, we can deduce a priori the signs of the first partial derivatives of q with respect to particular site characteristics. That is, we assume a priori knowledge of whether a particular site characteristic tends to make land more or less productive in any particular use. As the foregoing implies, each site has a different q value for each possible use; where it is necessary to distinguish the quality indices of a site in different uses, the notation q_j is adopted to denote the site's quality index in the jth industry.

The strategic value of introducing the q indices is that they allow us to handle analytically, in compact fashion, a number of site characteristics that determine the productivity of the site in various uses. In the empirical analysis, these indices will be replaced by quantitative measures of actual site characteristics. With this understanding, we may proceed to develop the equilibrium properties of the model.

III. The determinants of net density in a free market

The general form of the production function for the jth industry, as discussed above, is

$$X_j = F(K_j, L_j, q_jT_j),$$
$$\partial F/\partial V_i > 0, \quad V_i = K, L, qT, \quad (2.2)$$
$$\partial^2 F/\partial V_i^2 < 0, \quad V_i = K, L, qT,$$

where X_j is physical output (or H in the case of housing); and K_j, L_j, and T_j are inputs of capital, labor, and land (in acres).

However, for both theoretical and empirical analysis, it will be convenient to reduce the number of inputs to two, by assuming that housing services, H, are produced by capital and land alone, and that in other industries all nonland inputs are combined in fixed proportions so that nonland inputs can be denoted by a single variable N_j, a "bundle" of nonland factors.[3] Thus, the production function may be written

$$X = f(qT, N), \quad (2.2')$$

where the subscript j has been dropped to simplify the notation. Under constant returns to scale in N and qT, we have

$$X/T = f(q, N/T). \quad (2.3)$$

The value of output per acre, V/T, is obtained by multiplying

---

[3] This is, of course, a somewhat unrealistic assumption. However, it is undoubtedly true that the degree of substitution among nonland factors over the metropolitan area is of a much smaller order of magnitude than the degree of substitution between land and nonland factors. Moreover, for purposes of empirical analysis, reliable data are generally unavailable for more than one nonland input by industry.

III. The determinants of net density in a free market

Eq. (2.3) by the product price. Since product price is taken to be constant over the entire area, however, it is convenient to define the units of output so as to set price as equal to one in each industry. Thus

$$V/T = f(q, N/T), \qquad (2.4)$$

where the function, f, is now measured in dollar terms. Equation (2.4), then, is the gross revenue function, in density terms, for a firm in this industry. For a given value of q, say q', this function has the general shape of the curve in Figure 2.1. The ratio of nonland to land inputs, N/T, is, of course, the net density measure we seek to analyze.

The rental return per acre of land, R/T, is determined in a classical Ricardian fashion as the residual output per acre after all nonland factors of production have received their market returns. Since the prices of all nonland factors are assumed uniform over all sites and industries, rents will be

$$\begin{aligned} R/T &= f(q, N/T) - c(N/T), \\ &= R(q, N/T), \end{aligned} \qquad (2.5)$$

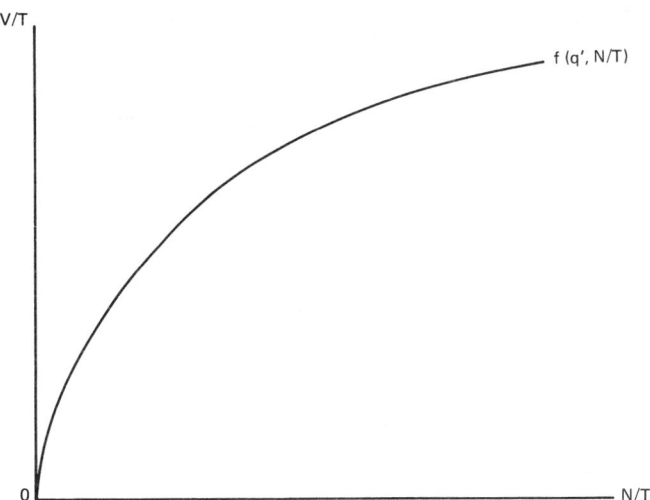

FIGURE 2.1. Production function for one quality of land.

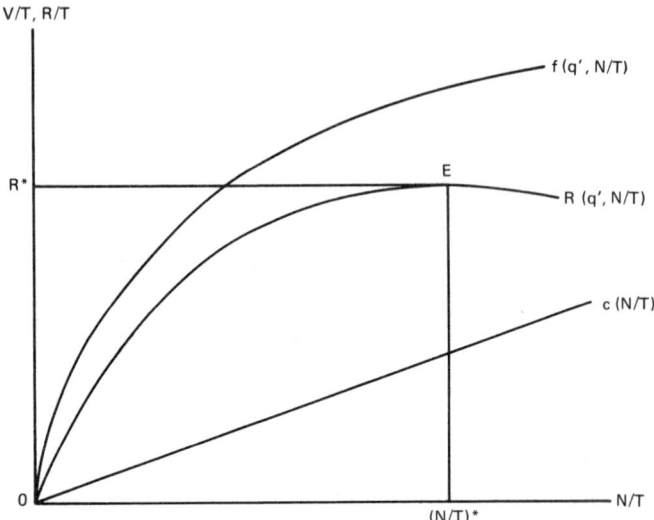

FIGURE 2.2. Derivation of equilibrium rent and net density.

where c is the price of a bundle of nonland factors and f is the revenue function. Land rent, then, is a function of the firm's net density and the quality of the site it occupies. This rent function is shown for one specific quality of land, q', in Figure 2.2 where the linear function $c(N/T)$ has been subtracted from the gross revenue function to yield the rent curve $R(q', N/T)$.

The firm itself (as distinct from the landowner) will be indifferent among the various combinations of rental return and net density along the rent curve, because everywhere along the curve nonland inputs receive their market return. The landowner, however, will seek to maximize the rental return to land so that competition among firms in the industry will force the rent for the site to the maximum point attainable on the rent curve, point E in Figure 2.2. If the tenant firm tried to operate at any other land use intensity, it would find itself outbid for the site by other firms in the industry willing to operate at the net density $(N/T)^*$, which maximizes land rent at the level R^*. The point $[(N/T)^*, R^*]$, then, is the equilibrium combination of net density and land rent for this industry on this quality of land.

III. The determinants of net density in a free market

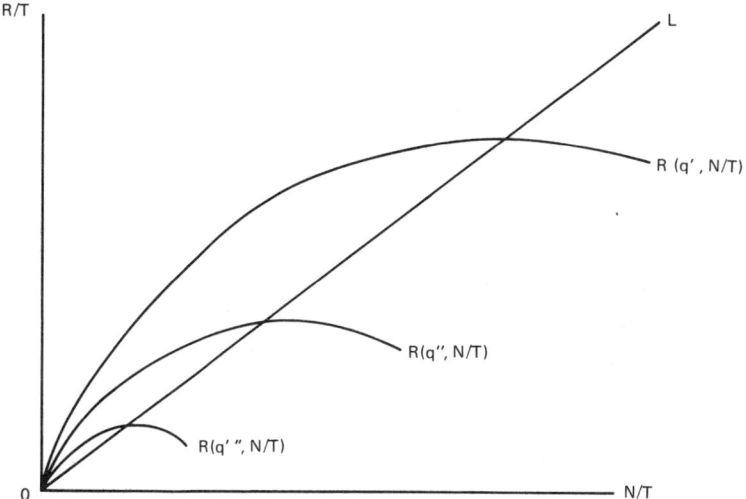

FIGURE 2.3. Equilibrium locus.

On other sites of different quality, of course, the same firm would have a different rent curve and thus a different equilibrium net density. Figure 2.3 shows several such rent curves. As already demonstrated, the equilibrium combination of net density and land rent for any one of these sites is at the point where that site's rent curve attains its maximum. By constructing the locus of all such maxima for all different qualities of land, we can map the complete set of possible equilibrium points; such an equilibrium locus is shown in Figure 2.3 as the line 0L. The points along 0L are the only combinations of net density and land rent that will be observable in equilibrium for firms in this industry, regardless of the quality of land upon which the firm is located.

Moreover, it can be readily shown that, given the revenue function of Eq. (2.4), the equilibrium locus 0L will be linear and proportional to net density. The first-order condition for a maximum along any particular rent function is obtained by setting the first partial derivative of Eq. (2.5) with respect to (N/T) equal to zero:

$$0 = \frac{\partial f(q, N/T)}{\partial(N/T)} - c$$

or (2.6)

$$\frac{\partial f(q, N/T)}{\partial(N/T)} = c.$$

This condition must hold for every point on the equilibrium locus. That is, the equilibrium locus is the set of rent–net density combinations corresponding to those points on the revenue functions for various qualities of land where the slope of the revenue function is equal to the price of a bundle of nonland inputs.

Under constant returns to scale,

$$\frac{\partial f(q, N/T)}{\partial(N/T)} = \frac{\partial f(1, N/qT)}{\partial(N/qT)}. \qquad (2.7)$$

Therefore,

$$\frac{\partial f(1, N/qT)}{\partial(N/qT)} = c. \qquad (2.8)$$

If the first partial derivative of f with respect to N/qT is to be a constant along the equilibrium locus, as required by Eq. (2.8), then N/qT must also be a constant. Dividing Eq. (2.4) by N/T, we have

$$(V/T)/(N/T) = (T/N)f(q, N/T), \qquad (2.9)$$

or, under constant returns to scale,

$$(V/T)/(N/T) = (qT/N)f(1, N/qT). \qquad (2.10)$$

If N/qT is constant along the equilibrium locus, as shown above, then by Eq. (2.10), $[(V/T)/(N/T)]$ is also a constant along the equilibrium locus. The slope of the equilibrium locus is $[(R/T)/(N/T)]$. By Eqs. (2.4) and (2.5),

III. The determinants of net density in a free market

$$R/T = V/T - c(N/T), \tag{2.11}$$

and

$$(R/T)/(N/T) = [(V/T)/(N/T)] - c, \tag{2.12}$$

or,

$$R/T = a(N/T), \tag{2.13}$$

where $a = [(V/T)/(N/T)] - c$, a constant. Thus, along the equilibrium locus, land rent per acre is a linear, proportional function of net density.

The relationships between the quality index, q, and both net density and land rent per acre can be derived similarly. By Eq. (2.10),

$$V/T = k_1 q, \tag{2.14}$$

where $k_1 = f(1, N/qT)$ is a constant since N/qT is a constant along the equilibrium locus. Substituting $k_1 q$ for V/T in Eq. (2.11),

$$R/T = k_1 q - c(N/T). \tag{2.15}$$

By Eq. (2.13),

$$N/T = (1/a)(R/T). \tag{2.16}$$

Substituting this value into Eq. (2.15) and solving for R/T,

$$R/T = [ak_1/(a + c)]q = kq. \tag{2.17}$$

Finally, Eqs. (2.16) and (2.17) imply

$$N/T = [k_1/(a + c)]q = Cq. \tag{2.18}$$

Thus, both land rent per acre and net density are linear, proportional functions of the quality index, q. The constants of proportionality k, C, and a in Eqs. (2.13), (2.17), and (2.18) are industry-specific. When it is necessary to distinguish these constants by industry, they will be written with industry subscripts.

Up to this point, we have not considered the effect of local property taxes upon the production decision. Property taxes can, however, be readily integrated into the model. For analytical purposes, it is convenient to consider separately the tax on land and nonland factors.

A proportional property tax on the value of the site itself will have no effect upon equilibrium net density; this is the classic case of a tax upon a perfectly inelastically supplied factor of production. In terms of the rent curves derived in Figures 2.2 and 2.3, such a tax simply results in a proportional downward shift of the entire rent curve, leaving the net density at which land rent (to the private landowner) attains a maximum unchanged.[4]

A proportional property tax on the value of capital improvements on the site (that is, on nonland inputs) will affect net density, however. A tax on improvements can be viewed as a component of the price of nonland factors. Thus, the slope of the linear cost function $c(N/T)$ in Figures 2.2 and 2.3 will be greater the greater is the tax on improvements. Specifically, if c is the cost of capital (or a bundle of nonland inputs) and t is

[4] Although property tax rates are normally defined in terms of land *value*, rather than land *rent*, it can easily be shown that, since land values are simply the present discounted value of future land rents, a tax that is proportional to land value is also proportional to land rent so long as rents are constant over time. If we denote market value per acre by V, the tax rate by t, the total tax per acre by T, gross rent per acre by R, and the discount rate by r, we have

$$T = tV = t(R - T/r).$$

Solving for T, we have

$$T = (t/r + t)R,$$

so that the tax per acre is proportional to gross rent per acre.

III. The determinants of net density in a free market

the tax per unit of capital (or per bundle of nonland inputs), the slope of the after-tax cost function will be $c(1 + t)$. Since the optimal net density is at the point where the slope of the revenue function is equal to the slope of the cost function, any increase in the slope of the cost function reduces the equilibrium net density of the site. Thus, net density will vary inversely with the tax rate, ceteris paribus. Introduction of the property tax leaves the equilibrium relationships of Eqs. (2.13), (2.17), and (2.18) unchanged, however, if the cost of nonland factors, c, is interpreted to include the tax on improvements and land rent per acre, R/T, is taken to be gross land rent, including that share of the return to land taken by the tax.

These three relationships are central to the theoretical model of this study and to the empirical estimation of the model. Taken together, they allow simultaneous estimation of the net density of land use and land rent for a municipality with given site characteristics.[5] Equation (2.18) is of particular interest because it shows that the equilibrium net density of a particular industry in a given locality can be determined solely on the basis of the site characteristics of the locality, given the parameters of the revenue function and the cost of nonland inputs. Thus, the market price of land does not enter into the determination of net density. This result is useful in interpreting the results obtained for the determination of gross densities in the following section.

At first, this result—that net density is independent of land rents—may appear to contradict economic intuition. Net density is the ratio of nonland to land inputs in the productive process, and one expects that relative factor inputs will, in general, depend on relative factor prices. If the price of land goes up, for

---

[5] Given the quality index, q, one of the three equations is, of course, redundant in the determination of net density and land rent. We make use of Eqs. (2.13) and (2.18) in the simultaneous estimation procedure of Chapter 4.

example, one might expect producers to economize by using less land relative to other inputs, that is, by increasing net density. It is important to bear in mind, however, that land rents are not determined entirely exogenously (from the standpoint of the firm) in the same way that other factor prices are. Land rent is the residual value of output after payments to all other factors. The equilibrium land rent determined above is the maximum residual that can be obtained with *any* combination of inputs. If the market price of land rises above this level—that is, if competing industries are, or become, able to bid more for the land than the firm in question—the firm will be forced to relinquish the site and move elsewhere. (The relationships derived here, of course, apply only for existing firms and the sites they actually occupy; they are actually observable equilibrium relationships.) On the other hand, market land rent cannot fall below the equilibrium level derived here; competition for the site from other firms in the same industry will assure that the land user must pay the maximum possible land rent for the site.

Thus, given the characteristics of the site, the firm's revenue function, and the prices of nonland inputs, equilibrium net density and land rent are uniquely determined. Changes in the market rental value of the site can occur only if other firms outbid the firm for the site; in which case, the firm will move to another site altogether.[6]

---

[6] Sir Ralph Hawtrey arrives at precisely the same conclusion (p. 118): "If we imagine him [the producer] reckoning how much land to use with a given force of labour and capital, and adding on successive hypothetical increments of land the price of an increment of land is irrelevant. . . . He pays the landlord the value of the cost-saving efficacy of the land, and for the land, apart from that characteristic, he pays what he would have to pay for marginal land, that is, nothing [Ralph Hawtrey, "Production Functions and Land: A New Approach," *The Economic Journal* 70(March 1960): 114–124]." Hawtrey's "cost-saving efficacy of the land" is very similar to the quality index introduced here.

IV. The determinants of areal shares in a free market

We turn now to the question alluded to at the end of the previous section: the competitive bidding process whereby sites are allocated to various land uses, that is, the determination of the areal shares of the various industries. Up to now, we have examined the equilibrium characteristics of the various land uses on the assumption that the firm in question has been successful in obtaining a particular site. The results of this analysis will be useful in determining the allocation of sites in a particular community among competing uses.

If sites are allocated by competitive bidding, a firm in the jth industry will be successful in obtaining a given site if

$$(R/T)_j > \max_{i \neq j}(R/T)_i, \qquad (2.19)$$

where $(R/T)_i$ is the equilibrium rent payable by a firm in the ith industry.[7] $\text{Max}(R/T)_i$ is simply the highest competing bid for the site. Using Eq. (2.17), this condition can be rewritten

$$k_j q_j > \max_{i \neq j} k_i q_i. \qquad (2.20)$$

If the site characteristics that determine q are taken to be exogenously determined and uniform over all sites within a given community, this allocation rule would imply that all sites within the community would be devoted to a single use, the

---

[7] The actual rent bids for the site will be, of course, the net (after-tax) rents obtainable in the various uses, rather than the gross rents indicated in Eq. (2.19). Since the proportional tax rate is assumed to be the same for all uses, however, the allocation criterion used here is completely equivalent to the corresponding criterion in terms of net rent bids.

use with the highest land-rental value for the existing combination of site characteristics. It is more realistic to suppose that the quality index for a given use depends, in part, upon the mix of other land uses in the community. In particular, it seems reasonable to suppose that there exists some degree of complementarity among the various land uses, so that the existence of other land uses in the community tends to increase the quality of sites for any particular use.[8] Thus, if we denote the areal share of total land in the community devoted to the jth use by p_j, we expect

$$\partial q_j/\partial p_i \geq 0, \quad \text{for all} \quad i \neq j. \tag{2.21}$$

Since the sum of areal shares over all industries must equal one, an increase in p_j implies a reduction in one or more of the p_i, $j \neq i$. In general, then, we expect

$$\partial q_j/\partial p_j \leq 0. \tag{2.22}$$

That is, an increase in the areal share devoted to the jth industry tends to reduce q_j by reducing the areal shares of complementary industries.

Given inequalities (2.21) and (2.22), the relation between $k_j q_j$ and max $k_i q_i$ will be of the general form shown in Figure 2.4. As indicated in Figure 2.4, there is a unique value of p_j, denoted $\bar{p}_j$, that insures that equality holds in the allocation rule

---

[8] For example, the existence of employment opportunities should increase the value of land in residential uses, and conversely, the existence of a large resident labor force in the community should increase the value of land in commercial and industrial uses. Similarly, complementarity should exist between retail trade and residential land uses. Of course, in some instances, one may expect the existence of one land use to reduce the attractiveness of sites for other land users; the case of low-income residential use is an obvious example. This possibility is viewed here as the exception, rather than the rule; however, the theoretical analysis developed in this section is quite capable of handling this case as well.

IV. The determinants of areal shares in a free market

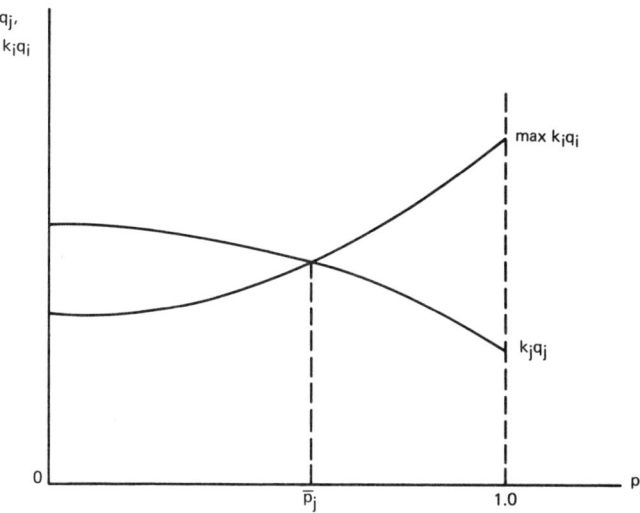

FIGURE 2.4. Equilibrium rents as functions of areal shares.

of (2.20). For any smaller value of p_j, the inequality holds and competitive bidding will expand the areal share of the jth industry. An areal share larger than $\bar{p}_j$, however, would result in competing industries being able to outbid industry j for some of its sites, reducing its areal share. Thus, the equilibrium areal share for the industry is $\bar{p}_j$.

The function $k_j q_j$ can, at least in principle, be estimated from observable empirical data. The maximum competing bid, max $k_i q_i$, is, however, an unobservable quantity; in those cases where the highest competing bid is an unsuccessful one, there is no market manifestation of its value. Therefore, for purposes of empirical estimation we shall simply use the market value of land as a proxy for competing bids. Denoting the market rental value of land in the community by $\bar{R}$, we have, then,

$$\bar{p}_j = \bar{p}_j(q_j, \bar{R}),$$
$$\partial \bar{p}_j / \partial q_j > 0, \qquad (2.23)$$
$$\partial \bar{p}_j / \partial \bar{R} < 0.$$

Substituting the expressions for net density and areal share contained in Eqs. (2.18) and (2.23) into the identity (2.1), we obtain the following expression for the gross density of the *j*th industry:

$$D_j = D_j(q_j, \bar{R}),$$
$$\partial D_j/\partial q_j > 0, \qquad (2.24)$$
$$\partial D_j/\partial \bar{R} < 0.$$

The signs of the first partial derivatives of D_j are unambiguously determined because both net density and areal share vary positively with q_j, and areal share varies negatively with $\bar{R}$ while net density is independent of $\bar{R}$, given q_j. Since the index q_j depends upon the areal shares of complementary land uses, as well as exogenously determined site characteristics, the set of *m* gross density functions for the various land uses, each of the form (2.24), are interdependent. We will recognize this interdependence in the empirical tests by estimating the *m* gross density functions as a set of simultaneous equations, with the gross density of one or more complementary land uses entering as an argument of the *q* index for each land use.

Under the simplifying assumption that the gross density functions are linear in land rents and the arguments of *q*, the basic set of equations to be estimated will have the form

$$D_j = b_0 + \sum_{i=1}^{n} b_i Z_i + \sum_{i \neq j} c_i D_i + b_{n+1} \bar{R}, \qquad j = 1, \ldots, m,$$
(2.25)

where the Z_i are exogenously determined site characteristics in the community, including governmental services and the local property tax rate. The estimation technique to be utilized is two-stage least squares, which provides consistent estimates of the parameters for a simultaneous equation system.

V. The effect of density zoning on gross density

The analysis developed so far assumes a perfectly competitive land market with each landowner free to select the use that maximizes his own private return. In reality, local governmental regulations impose important restrictions upon the uses to which sites may be devoted. The most significant restrictions are those imposed by local zoning ordinances, concerned both with type of use and density of use. Restrictions on the type of land use allowed on particular sites will not be considered here, partly because of the difficult conceptual problems involved and partly because of the lack of appropriate data for empirical testing. Maximum residential density (minimum lot size) regulations, however, can be easily introduced into the analysis. As noted in Chapter 1, density zoning may systematically discriminate against land uses (such as low-income housing) that are most profitable at high densities.

Since the impact of density zoning is usually discussed in terms of residential uses by income class, we shall conduct the analysis in those terms, although the results will be applicable to the allocation of land between housing and any competing use. For simplicity, let us consider just two types of housing. Figure 2.5 shows a hypothetical pair of rent curves for the two types of development, holding the quality of land constant. The rent curves are derived as in Section III, with rent per acre a function of net density. In the absence of lot size zoning, a site devoted to type 1 housing will be developed at net density d_1, yielding a land rent of r_1, while a site devoted to type 2 housing will have equilibrium net density and land rent d_2 and r_2. Under competitive bidding, land of this quality will be devoted to type 2 housing because it yields the higher equilibrium land rent.

Introduction of minimum lot size requirements may have one of several outcomes in this situation, depending upon the

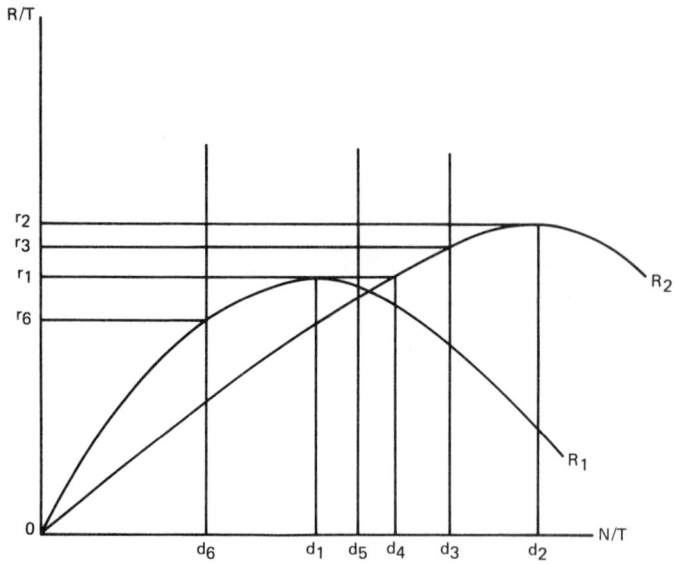

FIGURE 2.5. Effect of minimum lot zoning: Configuration 1.

level of the lot size requirement. Obviously, any minimum lot requirement that allows densities of d_2 or greater will have no effect upon the equilibrium outcome; such requirements are not binding. Suppose, however, the maximum allowable density is set at d_3. Then the maximum rent obtainable will be r_3, and the site will be devoted to type 2 housing at the maximum allowable density, d_3. In fact, any zoning regulation that allows densities of d_4 or greater will result in unchanged land use at either the maximum allowable density or density d_2, whichever is lower.

At densities below d_4, the return to type 2 development is less than r_1, so that if the maximum density is at some level d_5, less than d_4 but greater than d_1, the site will be developed for type 1 housing at density d_1 yielding land rent r_1. Finally, if the maximum density is set at some level d_6 less than d_1, type 1 housing will be built at density d_6, yielding a land rent of

V. The effect of density zoning on gross density

r_6, which is less than the free market equilibrium rent for that type of development.

We may summarize the results for this configuration of rent curves as follows:

1. If maximum allowable density exceeds d_2, land use, land rent, and net density are unaffected.
2. If maximum density is between d_4 and d_2, land use is unaffected but net density and land rent are reduced, as compared with the free market equilibrium; equilibrium net density will be the maximum allowable.
3. If maximum density is less than d_4, land use is changed to type 1 housing; equilibrium net density will be either the free market optimum for type 1 housing, d_1, or the maximum allowable density, whichever is lower. Land rents are reduced if the maximum allowable density is less than d_1.

We find, then, that binding minimum lot zoning may affect density and land rents without changing land use (case 2), or it may change both land use and density (case 3). The actual outcome will depend upon how stringent lot size requirements are.

The rent curve configuration in Figure 2.5 was, of course, arbitrarily determined; other configurations might imply different results. In particular, it is relevant to examine the case where the maximum return to type 2 housing, r_2, is less than r_1. Such a situation is illustrated in Figure 2.6. In this case, the equilibrium land use in a free market is type 1 housing, at density d_1 yielding land rent r_1. Here there is no minimum lot requirement that can change equilibrium land use; moreover, only if the maximum allowable density is less than d_1 will net density and land rent be affected.

If it is the objective of public policy to change land use from type 1 to type 2 under these conditions, the appropriate tool is maximum lot (minimum density) zoning. In practice, of course, this tool is virtually never applied because municipal authorities seldom wish to encourage dense residential devel-

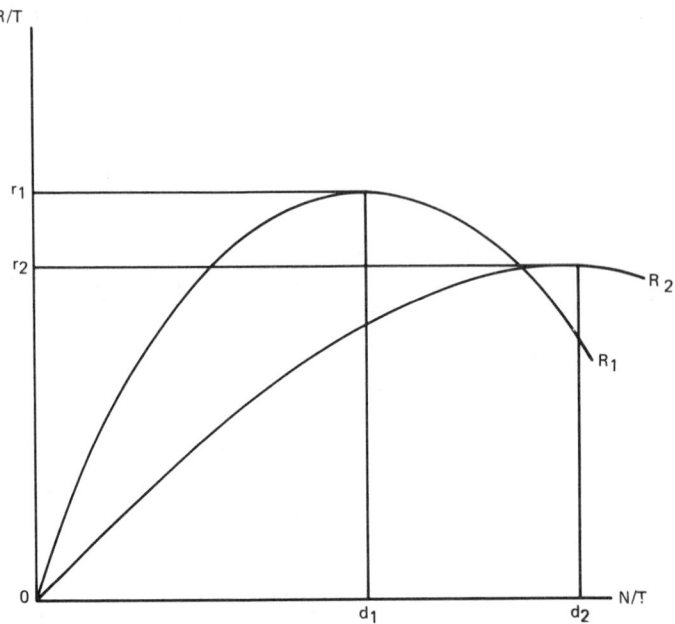

FIGURE 2.6. Effect of minimum lot zoning: Configuration 2.

opment. Alonso has suggested a social-policy rationale for application of maximum lot zoning, but its political feasibility is dubious.[9]

If, as we have assumed, the characteristics of housing may be associated with the income level of its occupants, we may interpret the results of this section in terms of household densities by income class. It is reasonable to suppose that the capital–land input ratio for low-income housing is greater than for high-income housing; this simply says that high-income households place a greater premium on space than do low-income households. Thus, we can interpret type 1 housing as high-income housing and type 2 housing as low-income housing.

Our results indicate that for each income class, minimum

[9] Alonso, *Location and Land Use*, p. 124.

VI. The market value of land

lot zoning, to the extent that it influences net density and land rent at all, reduces both. To the extent that zoning reduces land rent for a particular type of housing, it in turn reduces the profitability of that land use vis-à-vis nonresidential land use and therefore reduces the areal share of the community devoted to that land use. This reduction of areal share may be partially or wholly offset for the upper income groups, however, by their improved competitive position vis-à-vis other residential uses. Thus, we expect the net effect of binding minimum lot size zoning on gross density to be negative for low-income housing, and less strongly negative—or even positive—for high-income housing.

To test the effect of density zoning upon gross density of residential development by income class, a minimum lot size variable is included among the exogenous site characteristics (the Z_i) of the regression equations defined in Eq. (2.24). Although density zoning cannot, strictly speaking, be included in the arguments of the quality index, its effect upon gross density is, as we have seen, very similar; we shall therefore include it in the regression equations in the same fashion.

VI. The market value of land

It would not be legitimate to treat the value of land as an exogenously determined variable in a model that is designed to determine land use and, thus, land rents. Therefore, we now derive an expression for market land values that will allow the determination of land values as an endogenous variable of the model.

The particular land value variable that enters the model as a determinant of gross density is the average rental return to land in the municipality, which we shall denote by R. Average rent per acre may be expressed simply as an area-weighted sum of the rental return to land in the m different industries in the municipality:

$$R = \sum_{j=1}^{m} (T_j/T_0) \cdot R_j, \qquad (2.26)$$

where T_j and T_0 are, again, land devoted to the jth industry and total developed land in the municipality, respectively. Of course, if all land in the muncipality is valued at the same rent, the areal weights of R_j are immaterial; however, this formulation allows for the existence of varying qualities of land, and thus of rents, within the municipality. Using Eq. (2.13) to substitute for R_j, we can rewrite the last equation as

$$R = \sum_{j=1}^{m} (T_j/T_0) \cdot a_j(N/T)_j. \qquad (2.27)$$

Finally, using the definition of gross density in Eq. (2.1), we can write

$$R = \sum_{j=1}^{m} a_j D_j, \qquad (2.28)$$

where the D_j are gross densities and the a_j are the parameters of the equilibrium loci.

Equation (2.28) is of a form that can be utilized directly in regression analysis. Both R and D_j are directly observable, so that a linear regression may be used to estimate the a_j coefficients. Of course, since the gross density variables are also endogenous to the system, these coefficients must also be estimated by simultaneous equation regression.

3

Variables of the model

I. Land use categories

The theoretical model of Chapter 2 establishes certain testable relationships among land use densities, site characteristics, and land rents. In this chapter, the empirical variables that are employed to estimate these relationships are defined and discussed. The quality index of the theoretical model is specified to include measures of accessibility, the quality of municipal services, and housing conditions. In addition, gross density variables are defined for eight categories of land use, and measures of site costs, zoning restrictions, and property taxes are introduced. In Chapter 4 the theoretical model will be tested with data for these variables drawn from the Boston urban area.

Empirical research in this area is confronted by serious problems of data availability and variable specification. In some cases, such as land rents, empirical measures of the theoretically appropriate variable simply do not exist. In other cases, such as the quality of municipal services, it is difficult even to specify the theoretical concept in measurable form. In all cases, an attempt has been made to define empirical proxies that best capture the theoretical concepts of the model, subject to data availability.

An equation explaining gross density for each land use is included in the model developed in Chapter 2. In the empirical tests presented in Chapter 4, eight distinct land uses are considered: five residential and three nonresidential. Residential land use is divided into households with annual family income below $3000; $3000–$5999; $6000–$9999; $10,000–$24,999; and above $25,000.[1] The nonresidential classifications include manufacturing, retail trade, and professional and governmental services.

The gross density of each category of land use is measured in terms of nonland inputs per acre of developed land in the community. For residential uses, the input measure is the number of dwelling units occupied by households in the specified range. This is a proxy for the value of capital devoted to housing. For the nonresidential land uses, employment is used as the input measure.

In addition to the eight land use categories that enter the regression analysis as dependent variables, two aggregative land use densities enter as independent variables. Total residential gross density is used as a proxy for accessibility to labor and product markets within the community in the regression equations for nonresidential gross densities. Similarly, total employment gross density is included in the residential gross density equations as a measure of accessibility to employment opportunities within the community. Because these aggregative density measures are computed as the sums of the individual land

[1] Sources of data for all of the variables to be used in empirical estimation are presented in the Appendix.

II. Site costs

use gross densities defined above, they are treated in the estimation procedure as endogenous variables.

II. Site costs

In the theoretical model developed in Chapter 2, land rents are employed as a measure of the annual cost to the land user. For empirical analysis, however, annual land rents are generally unavailable, because typically, land is either occupied by the owner or rented together with the capital improvements on the site for a single rental fee. Fortunately, there are relatively good empirical measures of both the sale price of land and the rental value of land and improvements for rental properties, which may be used as site cost variables in the model.

As a measure of land values, we use the average assessed value of land per acre, adjusted by a sales-assessment ratio based on actual sales of land in the community. For the rental value of residential properties, we use the median gross monthly rent per room, calculated as the ratio of median rent per renter-occupied dwelling unit to the median number of rooms per dwelling unit. Gross rent, which includes the cost of utilities whether supplied by landlord or tenant, is used to standardize for differences among communities in the practice of provision of utilities. Rents are expressed in terms of rooms rather than dwelling units to standardize for differences in dwelling unit size among communities.

The land value variable will be employed as the measure of site costs in land uses that typically involve owner-occupancy (commercial, industrial, and high-income residential uses), while the rent variable will be used for land uses that typically involve renter-occupancy (low-income residential uses).[2]

---

[2] The distinction between high-income and low-income residential uses is based on an analysis of the proportion of rental housing

As noted in Chapter 2, site costs must be included as an endogenous variable of the model, since they are determined simultaneously with land use. Thus, the average price of land will be estimated within the model as a linear function of land use gross densities, as explained in that chapter. Similarly, residential rents will be estimated as a linear function of other variables of the model.

III. Quality characteristics

The quality index, q, is assumed to depend upon such community characteristics as the quality of local governmental services in the community and accessibility to other economic activities. The specific variables used as proxies for these community characteristics are defined in the following.

---

by income class in the Boston SMSA. A conservative estimate of the percentage of renters in the household income classes defined for this study, as of 1960, is as follows: for the income range below $3000, 55 percent; for the range $3000–$5999, 61 percent; for the range $6000–$9999, 48 percent; and for incomes above $10,000, 32 percent.

Data for homeowner incomes are available only for single-family dwellings; 90 percent of all dwelling units were single-family homes, so the number of single-family homeowner dwelling units in each income class was multiplied by 1.11 and expressed as a percentage of households (families and unattached persons) in that income range. The resulting estimates probably overstate the number of homeowner households in the lower income classes, and possibly in all income classes, insofar as multiple-family dwelling units tend more often to be commercial, nonhomeowner properties than do single-family homes, and the average income of homeowners living in multiple-family dwellings is probably higher than for homeowners in single-family dwellings. Data for homeowner properties are taken from U. S. Bureau of the Census, *U. S. Census of Housing, 1960*, Vol. V, "Residential Finance," Part 1 (Washington, D. C.: U. S. Government Printing Office): 144; households by income class from U. S. Bureau of the Census, *U. S. Census of Population, 1960*, Vol. I, Part 23 (Massachusetts), Table 76 (Washington, D. C.: U. S. Government Printing Office).

Accessibility variables

The dominant feature of most of the theoretical treatments of urban location is the emphasis on accessibility to product and factor markets. Residential location is viewed as being strongly influenced by the distribution of employment opportunities and the cost, in time and money, of commuting to work. Conversely, the spatial distribution of industrial and commercial activity is assumed to be influenced by the distribution of the potential labor force and the product markets. In most of the existing abstract theoretical models, however, all nonresidential activities are assumed to be concentrated at the center of the metropolitan area, often at a single point. Accessibility to employment in such models can be represented as simply the distance to the central business district. Any model designed for empirical testing must include a more general measure of accessibility, one capable of describing the decentralization of employment, labor force, and markets that exists in reality.

The model tested here will include two general types of accessibility measures. Accessibility to employment, labor, and markets within the community will be represented by total gross density of employment and residential land use in the community, as indicated earlier. As an index of accessibility to economic activity in other communities, a variable of the following form will be introduced:

$$A_i = \sum_{j \neq i} (E_j/t_{ij}^2), \qquad (3.1)$$

where E_j is employment in the jth community ($j \neq i$), and t_{ij} is the highway travel time between the ith and the jth communities.

This measure of accessibility is one of the so-called "potential" indices, which have been widely used in recent years by empirical investigators in the fields of urban and spatial economics and ecology. Unfortunately, the premises from which such an index derives are more heuristic than theoretical; however, its utility as a compact quantitative measure of the whole complex spatial distribution of urban activities is such as to recommend its use, despite its lack of theoretical rigor. The basic notion underlying the potential index is that the influence exerted by economic activity in one community upon another community will vary directly with the level of the activity (here represented by employment) and inversely with the distance or travel time between the two communities. The index defined above arbitrarily assumes that this influence decreases with the square of highway travel time.[3] It is further assumed that the separate effects of employment in outlying communities on the ith community are additive, so that the total potential created in the ith community is simply the summation of the E_j/t_{ij}^2 terms for the other n communities. The index, of course, is not defined for $t_{ij} = 0$, so the ith community itself cannot be included in the index. Hence, gross employment density within the community must be included along with the potential index as a measure of employment opportunities within the community, as explained earlier.

Originally, it was intended that indices would be included in the model as measures of accessibility to a number of different activities, such as retail trade, different types of employment, and labor supplies of various types. Obviously, the importance in locational decisions of accessibility to these various activities differs depending on whether the decisions concern business firms or households. Similarly, the value of accessi-

---

[3] Attempts to estimate directly the value of this "distance exponent" (here assumed equal to 2.0) have resulted in a wide range of values, depending upon the type of interaction and geographic region considered. For example, Carroll found values ranging from 2.83 to 3.36, while Ikle estimated exponents ranging from .7 to 2.6. J. Douglas Carroll, "Spatial Interaction and the Urban Metropolitan Regional Description," *Regional Science Association Proceedings:* 1(1955); F. C. Ikle, "Sociological Relationship of Traffic to Population and Distance," *Traffic Quarterly* (April 1954).

III. Quality characteristics

bility to a particular activity may vary with the characteristics of the firm or household. As it turned out, however, all of these indices were so highly correlated (zero-order correlations of .96 to .99) that inclusion of more than one in the model would add little explanatory power while raising serious problems of collinearity among the independent variables. For this reason, accessibility to employment as defined earlier was selected as a generalized accessibility variable to serve as a proxy for other types of activity as well. Thus, this variable is used in both the residential and the industrial regressions of Chapter 4.

Municipal services

There are a number of municipal services that may significantly affect the quality of sites within any particular community. The task of accurately quantifying the quality of such services empirically is, however, a difficult one. The most readily available data relating to local public services are expenditure data, but expenditures may not accurately reflect the quality of services provided if the costs of service provision vary from one community to another. While recognizing this fact, we are forced to rely upon expenditure variables for several of the more important municipal functions, for want of a better quality index. These variables must be interpreted, then, as only rough approximations of the true quality of local services.

Table 3.1 presents a summary of the major categories of expenditures of local governments in Massachusetts for 1962. These figures are helpful in selecting those municipal services that may be expected to influence location decisions.

Public education. Judged solely on the basis of volume of expenditure, public education is by far the most important single service provided by local governments, accounting for approximately 40 percent of local expenditures. Intuitively, one also expects the quality of public education to be the principal municipal service influencing location decisions, at least for

TABLE 3.1

Revenues and expenditures of local governments in Massachusetts, 1962 (in $1000s; expenditure items under $20,000,000 omitted)

Revenue		1,154,028
From own sources		
Property taxes	861,341	
Current charges	91,324	
Special assessments	3,991	
Other	197,372	
Utility revenue		132,894
Intergovernmental revenue		345,499
Expenditures, by function		
Education		484,058
Highways		91,998
Fire protection		70,192
Police protection		68,563
Sewerage and sanitation		51,499
Parks and recreation		22,750
Utilities (power, water, gas, and transit)		136,721
General control and administration, public buildings, and interest		83,298
Public welfare		184,371
Health and hospitals		63,223
Housing and urban renewal		46,963
Insurance trust (retirement)		37,402

Source: *1962 U. S. Census of Governments,* Vol, 7, No. 21, p. 25.

households. Two alternative measures of the quality of public education are tested in the empirical analysis: annual expenditures per pupil (excluding capital outlays) and the pupil–teacher ratio.

Public streets and highways. A second municipal service that may have an important influence upon location decisions is the extent and quality of public streets and highways. Residents may be assumed to be concerned with the quality of streets

III. Quality characteristics

near their homes, and business firms, especially retail establishments, will be concerned with the ease of access of pedestrian and vehicular traffic to their premises. The variable selected for empirical analysis is annual current expenditures on streets and highways per developed acre in the community. This variable incorporates both the extent and quality of the street network, since it is the product of expenditure per mile of streets and miles of streets per developed acre.

Fire and police protection. The quality of fire and police protection will determine the security of persons and property in the community. Expenditures for these functions are unlikely to be good measures of their quality, however, since the cost of providing a given level of security undoubtedly varies greatly among communities. The quality variables to be used for these services, therefore, are standardized fire and burglary insurance premiums in the various communities. Fire insurance companies in Massachusetts classify cities and towns into seven rate categories, based solely on technical aspects of local fire protection. Among the factors taken into account are adequacy of water supply, fire department equipment and personnel, alarm system, fire prevention measures, and the municipal building department. The variable used as a measure of quality of fire protection is the annual insurance premium for $20,000 single-family, brick and frame homes in each community.

A variable similar to that used to measure the quality of fire protection is available for the measurement of police protection. Premiums for burglary insurance on industrial property in Massachusetts are calculated in much the same way as fire insurance premiums, with communities again divided into seven rate classifications. In the case of burglary insurance, however, the community's rate classification depends in part upon its past record of such crimes, as well as upon the quality of municipal law enforcement. Thus, burglary-insurance rate differentials will reflect both factors that are within the control of local government (the quality of law enforcement) and factors that are not (socioeconomic conditions that give rise to crime). Still, it would seem that the relevant consideration from a locational standpoint is the risk of sustaining loss from burglary; insurance rates are probably a good proxy for this. We are implicitly assuming that protection against all crimes against persons and property is highly correlated with burglary protection, which is the only kind of protection we can quantify.[4] The particular insurance premium used is the annual rate on $100,000 worth of prime-risk industrial property.

Publicly provided water, and sewerage and sanitation services. The next municipal service in Table 3.1, sewerage and sanitation services, is one for which quality differentials are unlikely to be important enough to affect location decisions significantly, with the exception of those communities that fail to provide the service at all. It was decided, therefore, to use a dummy variable for those communities that fail to provide public sewerage facilities. Also incorporated into this dummy variable are those communities that do not have a public water supply. The dummy variable, then, is 0.0 for communities that provide both water and sewerage and 1.0 for those that lack one or the other. The two services are combined to obtain a meaningful amount of variance within the empirical sample (only six of the thirty-one municipalities lack one or the other) and to economize on the number of independent variables. Among those communities that do provide these facilities, a variety of financial procedures are practiced; some communities levy special assessments for capital outlays while others do not, and some charge for water consumption while others do not. Thus, the use of a dummy variable implicitly assumes that even if the land user is assessed some charge for publicly provided facilities, the cost

[4] A more general measure of crime incidence and police protection is the per capita crime rate for various classes of crime; unfortunately, such statistics are unavailable for the smaller towns in the sample region.

III. Quality characteristics

will be small compared to what it would cost to provide the service himself.

Public parks and recreation. The expenditures for parks and recreation shown in Table 3.1 probably greatly understate the real value of this municipal service. First, current outlays do not include the imputed value of land and fixed capital devoted to parks. Almost certainly, the aesthetic contribution of parks and green spaces to the residential amenities of a community vastly exceeds the small annual maintenance cost required.

Unfortunately, expenditure data are virtually the only available quantitative measure of these services and are therefore the measure that is used. To standardize for community size, this variable is expressed as annual current expenditures on parks and recreation per developed acre in the community.[5]

Other municipal services. For several reasons, none of the rest of the municipal services included in Table 3.1 are considered in our empirical analysis. Public utilities other than water, for example, are probably not influential in location decisions. As indicated by the revenue and expenditure figures in Table 3.1, these services are normally provided at prices approximating full cost. Unlike water and sewers, however, if not provided publicly these utilities (electricity, gas, and transit) are usually available from private producers at comparable prices.

The regulatory and governing activities represented by the expenditures on general control and administration, public buildings, and interest are excluded, not because the overall quality of municipal administration is not an important amenity but because it is almost impossible to quantify.

---

[5] Per capita expenditures on parks and recreation were also computed and tried in the regressions of Chapter 4. In general, the results were very similar; however, expenditures per developed acre gave generally more significant results than the per capita measure. The correlation between the two variables is .65.

The remaining expenditure categories in Table 3.1—public welfare, health and hospitals, housing and urban renewal, and pension payments—are mainly redistributive transfer payments, which are not well suited to inclusion in the model. Whatever effect these expenditures might have on the location of population or industry would undoubtedly be swamped by the reverse effect of the composition of population in the community upon the level of the expenditures themselves. The density of low-income households, for example, could be expected to be highly correlated with welfare expenditures, not necessarily because low-income households are attracted by them but because low-income households generate the need for such expenditures.

Condition of housing

An important, but often intangible, consideration in the location decision of most households is one that might be loosely called the "character" of the neighborhood or community. This rather general term encompasses a wide variety of community characteristics, many of which cannot be precisely quantified. Among the most important, however, are aesthetic considerations having to do with the architecture, condition, and layout of physical structures. To capture at least one dimension of community character, we utilize an index of the condition of dwelling units in the community. This index is defined as the percent of dwelling units classified as dilapidated or deteriorating by the *U. S. Census of Housing*.

This housing condition index enters into the model in two distinct ways. First, it is used as a measure of external diseconomies created for people living in the community who do not inhabit such substandard dwellings. Presumably, the existence of run-down housing nearby reduces the attractiveness of even those homes that are in good condition. Thus, the index is included in the gross density regressions for upper-income residence as a measure of amenities in the community.

IV. Minimum zoned lot size

Such an index, however, cannot legitimately be used to predict gross densities of those income groups that are likely to inhabit dilapidated or deteriorating housing. The gross density of low-income residence is very highly correlated with the index of substandard housing; however, this is not because these households are attracted by poor quality housing (despite the numerous references in the literature to the "demand for poor quality housing"). Low-income households are, however, attracted by cheap housing, which often turns out to be poor quality housing. The second way in which the housing condition index enters the model, therefore, is as an explanatory variable in the regression for median gross rent per room. We expect that the estimated regression coefficient will be negative, indicating that poor quality housing brings lower rents.

IV. Minimum zoned lot size

As explained in Chapter 2, local governments may affect land use through their power to regulate land use density, particularly via residential density zoning. Such regulations, if binding, will affect residential net densities and may affect areal shares by income class. It is therefore necessary to include a measure of the stringency of density zoning regulations in the residential land use gross density regressions.

Unfortunately (from the standpoint of the empirical investigator), actual lot size zoning regulations are not so simple as those depicted in our model, at least at the municipal level. Most cities and towns prescribe several residential zones with a different minimum lot requirement in each zone. This need not unduly vitiate our approach, however. Zones with different lot size requirements will do no more than segregate residential development within the community by income class so long as the zone with maximum allowable density is sufficiently large to accommodate all the low-income development that would have taken place anyway, and the lot size required in that zone is not binding. Since most of the municipalities with stringent zoning regulations are suburban communities with a good deal of undeveloped land in nearly all residential zones, the crucial variable would seem to be the lot size requirement of this most permissive zone. Moreover, to the exent that the entire structure of lot size requirements tends to move together from community to community (and inspection of the zoning requirement indicates that it does), this *minimum minimorum* is a good proxy for the entire structure of lot size requirements. Therefore, the variable we have selected for empirical testing is the absolute minimum lot size required anywhere in the community, expressed in square feet.

V. Property taxes

As demonstrated in Chapter 2, taxation of capital improvements tends to reduce both net density and equilibrium land rents. Thus, we expect property taxation to reduce gross densities in all land uses via its effect on net density and to discriminatorily reduce the areal share of capital-intensive uses, where its effect on equilibrium land rents will be strongest. Moreover, since tax rates vary from one community to another, we expect gross land use densities to respond to these differentials as well, with capital-intensive uses being discouraged in high-tax communities.

To measure these effects, we introduce an equalized tax rate variable in the gross density equations. The tax rate variable that is used is the nominal tax rate on assessed value, multiplied by the estimated ratio of assessed to market value, based on current market sales of taxable property.

Property tax rates may be included directly in the gross density regressions for uses that typically involve owner occupancy (nonresidential and high-income residential uses). However, for predominately renter-occupied residential properties, a different procedure is followed. Tax rates are assumed

V. Property taxes

to affect gross densities in these uses only indirectly, via their effects upon residential rents; the property tax rate is entered as an independent variable in the estimation of residential rents, which, in turn, is entered in the gross density regressions for households with incomes below $10,000.

The rationale for this procedure is that tax rate differentials among communities can affect the gross density of rental housing only to the extent that they are reflected in rent differentials, that is, only if the tax differential is shifted forward to the land uses. The theoretical conditions for forward shifting of such differentials are well established.[6] In the short run, where the supply of capital improvements in the community is fixed, the tax falls entirely upon the return to capital; that is, the return to capital falls by the full amount of the tax, and the market value of capital is lowered by the capitalized value of all future tax liabilities. Over the longer run, however, as capital has time to adjust to the tax, this depressed rate of return to capital tends to discourage new investment and replacement, and the supply of capital contracts, raising the gross and net return to capital. In the long run, if the supply of capital in the community is perfectly elastic, the gross return to capital rises by the full amount of the tax and the tax is fully shifted forward to renters via higher rents, provided that the demand for capital services is sufficiently inelastic to permit the necessary increase in rents. Even in the intermediate run, the elasticity of demand governs the degree of contraction of the housing stock required to effect a given degree of tax shifting. Thus, both the elasticity of supply and the elasticity of demand influence the degree of tax shifting; elastic supply and inelastic demand tend to favor shifting, while inelastic supply and elastic demand tend to reduce shifting.

---

[6] Theoretical aspects of the shifting of residential property taxes are discussed in greater detail by this author in "The Incidence of Differential Property Taxes on Urban Housing," *National Tax Journal* 21(September 1968): 253–262.

In the present context, we can make several a priori observations about these elasticities that may be particularly relevant. First, in the case of urban housing, the long run may be very long indeed. The long life and immobility of residential capital, together with the slow rate of change of the housing stock, argue for a relatively inelastic supply function, at least over the period for which tax rate and tax differentials may be assumed stable.[7] Moreover, it is important to note that the demand function that is relevant for the analysis of shifting of tax *differentials* is the demand for housing *in the particular community* in question. At the community level, the demand for housing services may be expected to be relatively elastic because of the existence of many comparable alternative locations in communities nearby; this will tend to minimize the shifting of intercommunity tax differentials if the supply of capital is less than perfectly elastic. These considerations, then, point toward substantially less than full shifting of tax differentials and indicate that the impact of tax differentials on residential location may be small.

It must be recognized, of course, that the impact of property tax differentials on location may be offset to some extent by the advantages conferred by the municipal services provided from tax revenues. That is, communities with higher tax rates— and higher rents, if there is shifting—may also provide higher

[7] In the Boston SMSA in 1959, 80 percent of all dwelling units were in structures built before 1940, according to the U. S. Bureau of the Census, *U. S. Census of Housing, 1960*, "Components of Inventory Change," Part 1A, Boston Area (Washington, D. C.: U. S. Government Printing Office): 19. For the period 1950–1959, the average annual gross increment to the housing stock was about 2.2 percent, of which 1.5 percent was due to new construction and 7 percent was the net effect of conversion of existing dwelling units, while the average annual rate of removals from the housing stock for the period was about 1.0 percent, according to the U. S. Bureau of the Census, *U. S. Census of Housing, 1960*, "Components of Inventory Change," Part 1B, Boston Area (Washington, D. C.: U. S. Government Printing Office): 15.

V. Property taxes

quality services. Just as the capitalization of tax liabilities into housing values will tend to depress the return to capital, the capitalization of service benefits will tend to enhance property values and the return to capital. We can test for this effect by the inclusion of municipal service quality variables in both the residential gross density regressions and the residential rent regression. A significant relationship between service quality differentials and rent levels in the latter function would be evidence of some capitalization of municipal services into rents and property values. Unfortunately, it is difficult to define exactly what "full" capitalization of service differentials would mean, since there is no unambiguous way to assign dollar values to service quality differentials.

The supply condition that might be expected to result in capitalization of service quality differentials is precisely the same as that required for capitalization of tax differentials: inelasticity of supply of housing, resulting in the bidding-up of capital values in favorable locations. It is not true, however, that full capitalization of both tax and service differentials would necessarily result in a "neutral" situation in which rent differentials exactly match property tax differentials. This is because there is no unique relationship between service benefits per household and tax rates. Tax rates depend not only on service expenditures but also on the size of the tax base, which often includes a good deal of nonresidential property. Even if service expenditures are a good measure of service quality, the tax rate necessary to support a given level of services per household will vary widely with variations in the tax base per household, that is, with the ratio of nonresidential to residential property in the tax base.[8] At one extreme is the industrial enclave where high quality services to households are possible at very low tax

---

[8] Inspection of the zero-order correlations between tax rates and the measures of service quality defined above, for the sample region, bear out this observation; these correlations are uniformly low, on the order of 0 to 0.30.

rates; at the other extreme is the nonindustrial bedroom suburb where households must "pay their own way."[9] Thus, full capitalization of both taxes and services may result in the owner recouping either more or less than the full property tax differential through differentially higher rent or property value.

[9] Data on taxable property values per capita and property tax rates for 279 taxing units in nine counties in northeastern New Jersey presented by Morris Beck in Appendix C of *Property Taxation and Urban Land Use: Interaction of Local Taxes and Urban Development in the Northeastern New Jersey Metropolitan Region* (Washington, D. C.: Urban Land Institute, 1963) show a range of equalized values per capita in 1960 of 32:1 and a range of property tax rates of 7:1.

4

Empirical tests of the model

I. The nature of the sample and estimation technique

The metropolitan region on which the model developed in Chapters 2 and 3 is to be tested is the Boston area. The sample region corresponds roughly to what the *1960 U. S. Census of Population* defines as the Boston "urbanized area," a region somewhat smaller than the standard metropolitan statistical area. Not all of the cities and towns in that area were included in the sample because for some the necessary data were not available; sufficient data were available for thirty-one cities and towns in, or contiguous to, the Boston urbanized area, so they make up our sample.[1] To give the reader some idea of the nature of the sample, these communities are listed in Table 4.1 together with their 1960 population and median family income. Comparison of the data collected for this study with corresponding figures for municipalities not in the sample indicates that the thirty-one municipalities selected for analysis provide a representative cross-section, in terms of geography, size of population, and socioeconomic characteristics of the region.

The model, as developed in Chapters 2 and 3, is a cross-sectional model, requiring concurrent data for all variables. Unfortunately, concurrent data are not available for all the variables that analysis suggests are important, so the actual data used span the period 1959–1963. For any one variable, of course, the observations are entirely concurrent over the sample region. This inconsistency should not greatly vitiate the regression results because inspection of earlier data indicates that the relative magnitudes of most variables do not change greatly over periods of this length.[2]

[1] The principal data constraints encountered were the lack of detailed census data for the smaller towns in the region and the lack of data on the market value of land for a fairly random subset of cities and towns. (See the description of data sources in the Appendix.)

[2] Sources of the data to be used are described in detail in the Appendix. In general, all data relating to characteristics of population and housing stock are from the U. S. Bureau of the Census, *U. S. Census of Population, 1960* and the U. S. Bureau of the Census, *U. S. Census of Housing, 1960;* data on land use, employment, and travel times were collected by the Boston Regional Planning Project of the Massachusetts Department of Public Works, for the year 1963; land values were calculated from data supplied by the Massachusetts Department of Corporations and Taxation, for 1962; minimum zoned lot size and educational expenditures per pupil for 1960–1961 are from *Town and City Monographs,* a publication of the Massachusetts Department of Commerce; the remaining categories of municipal expenditures are from the U. S. Bureau of the Census, *U. S. Census of Government, 1962* (Washington, D. C.: U. S. Government Printing Office); and equalized property tax rates were calculated by the Massachusetts Federation of Taxpayers Association, for 1962.

TABLE 4.1

Sample communities

Community	Population	Median family income
Andover	17,704	$ 7,694
Belmont	27,573	8,372
Boston	670,940	5,747
Braintree	34,593	4,474
Brookline	54,100	8,380
Cambridge	104,054	5,923
Chelsea	33,187	5,298
Dedham	24,600	7,554
Everett	44,535	5,983
Hingham	16,911	8,149
Holbrook	11,165	6,903
Lynnfield	9,784	9,413
Malden	55,790	6,194
Marblehead	21,613	7,967
Medford	69,552	6,693
Melrose	29,920	7,507
Newton	89,683	9,008
Norfolk	3,488	5,982
Peabody	44,694	6,749
Quincy	89,075	6,785
Randolph	20,421	6,880
Rockland	15,296	6,273
Saugus	22,647	6,978
Somerville	95,650	6,024
Swampscott	13,966	7,967
Wakefield	26,609	6,695
Watertown	40,046	7,003
Wellesley	26,264	11,478
Westwood	11,895	8,690
Winthrop	20,294	6,573
Woburn	37,420	6,650

Source: U. S. Department of Commerce, Bureau of the Census, *1960 U. S. Census of Population,* Vol. I, Pt. 23 (Massachusetts), Table 32 and Table 76.

The estimation technique utilized throughout this section, unless otherwise indicated, is two-stage least squares regression.[3] As noted in Chapters 2 and 3, the determination of land use densities and land values must be considered as a simultaneous system. Parameters estimated by ordinary single-equation least squares will, in general, be biased if any of the explanatory variables are determined simultaneously with the dependent variable. Two-stage least squares estimates have the property of consistency; that is, in the limit, as sample size approaches infinity, they are unbiased.[4]

Before going on to a discussion of the results of estimation, we should consider the interpretation of results obtained from a cross-sectional sample such as this. The model developed here assumes long-run equilibrium of all activities. Thus, the policy effects measured are assumed to be those observable in long-run equilibrium; changes in the policy parameters will have the predicted effect only after all activities have had time to adjust fully to the change. Unfortunately, there is no way to estimate the time required for this adjustment, short of formulating a fully dynamic model.

In assuming that the empirical observations represent long-

---

[3] Briefly, the estimation of a single equation is carried out as follows. In the first stage, each of the independent variables that is endogenous to the model is estimated by ordinary least squares as a function of all the exogenous variables of the system. In the second stage, the endogenous variables are then replaced by their first-stage estimates and the parameters of the equation are estimated by ordinary least squares. The purpose of the technique is to purge the explanatory variables of any variation except that which can be explained by the exogenous variables of the model; in effect, the dependent variable is estimated as a function of the exogenous variables alone, since the endogenous variables have been replaced by linear functions of the exogenous variables.

[4] John J. Johnston, *Econometric Methods* (New York: McGraw-Hill, 1963), p. 262.

I. The nature of the sample and estimation technique

run equilibrium, we implicitly assume that the values of the exogenous variables have been static for a long enough period for all endogenous variables to adjust to their equilibrium levels. Of course, in reality there is continual change in the values of these variables. There are, however, good grounds for the presumption that the relative values of these variables from community to community change only slowly. To test the stability of intercommunity differentials, data were obtained for earlier years for several of the exogenous variables, and the simple correlation between the sample observations and an average of earlier observations was calculated. The variables tested in this manner were equalized property tax rates and the two measures of quality of public education, educational expenditures per pupil and the pupil–teacher ratio. In testing equalized property tax rates, an unweighted average of 1956, 1959, and 1962 property tax rates was correlated with the 1962 rates that were used in the estimation procedure. In testing the quality of education variables, an unweighted average of levels for both measures of quality for the academic years 1954–1955, 1957–1958, and 1960–1961 was correlated with the 1960–1961 levels. For tax rates the zero-order correlation was .95; for educational expenditures per pupil it was .93; and for the pupil–teacher ratio the correlation was .89. These high correlations indicate a remarkable stability of intercommunity differentials, even though for two of the three variables (tax rates and educational expenditures) there were relatively large changes (on the order of 10 to 25 percent) in the average absolute level of the variable. It is felt that this degree of stability in the exogenous variable over a seven-year period justifies the assumption of substantially full adjustment of economic activities to intercommunity differentials.

On the basis of this evidence, it was also deemed unnecessary to introduce lagged values of the exogenous variables. Instead, current values are used on the assumption that these reflect long-term intercommunity differentials.

II. Preliminary tests of the model

Before discussing the estimation of the land use gross density regressions, it is useful to present several empirical tests of the theory developed in Chapter 2. Equations (2.13) and (2.18), demonstrating the proportionality between net density and land rents, and between net density and the quality index, q, may be estimated empirically, at least at an aggregative level. The equations for the jth industry are

$$(R/T)_j = a_j(N/T)_j, \qquad (2.13)$$

$$(N/T)_j = Cq_j, \qquad (2.18)$$

where $(R/T)_j$ is equilibrium rent per acre and $(N/T)_j$ is equilibrium net density.

The calculation of net density requires data for the area of land in the community devoted to the use in question; such data are available only for the categories of all employment and all residence. Equations (2.13) and (2.18) were therefore estimated by ordinary least squares for these two aggregative categories of land use. Net employment density, N_E, was expressed as employees per employment acre; net residential density, N_R, as households per residential acre; and land values, P, as average market price per acre of land in the community, in $1000 units. The regression results are

$$P = 4.12 + 1.75N_R$$
$$ (1.55) \quad (4.46) \qquad (4.1)$$

$$R^2 = .41$$

and

$$P = .18 + .04N_E$$
$$ (.07) \quad (5.91) \qquad (4.2)$$

$$R^2 = .55.$$

II. Preliminary tests of the model

Both the estimated coefficients of net density are significant at the 99 percent confidence level, as indicated by the t-tests of significance (in parentheses).[5] Moreover, the constant in the employment density equation is virtually zero, indicating that the regression line passes through the origin, just as required by the theoretical analysis.

A more refined version of the net residential density equation was also estimated in an attempt to take account of the extreme heterogeneity of the types of households included in "all residence." Since data are not available to calculate net densities by individual income class, an income variable, Y, the fraction of households with income over $10,000, was included as an independent variable to standardize for the varying socioeconomic composition of different communities. The estimated equation is

$$P = -6.05 + 2.16N_R + 33.23Y$$
$$(-1.16) \quad (5.23) \quad (2.21) \quad\quad (4.3)$$
$$R^2 = .50.$$

Again, the regression coefficients are significant at high levels of confidence, and the constant is now not significantly different from zero. The inclusion of the income variable also markedly increased the overall fit of the equation. Taken together, Eqs. (4.2) and (4.3) substantiate the theoretical proposition of a linear, proportional relationship between net density and land values. Although the regressions leave a substantial fraction of the variation of land values unexplained, it must be borne in mind that this is a fairly crude test of the theory. Both the em-

---

[5] Chemical Rubber Company, *Standard Mathematical Tables*, "Table for t-Test of Significance" (Cleveland, Ohio: Chemical Rubber Company, 1957), p. 244. For 25 degrees of freedom, a t-statistic of 1.71 or greater indicates that the coefficient is significantly different from zero at about the 95 percent level of confidence; a t-statistic of 1.0 or greater indicates significance at about the 85 percent level of confidence.

ployment and residential categories are heterogenous aggregations of the industries assumed in the theory; the inclusion of an income variable in the residential equation standardizes for this heterogeneity only to a first approximation. Moreover, the value of land in a particular use may differ systematically from the average price of land in the community. Finally, the actual data used for land values are based upon equalized assessed values, which are subject to measurement errors.

The theoretical conclusion that net density may be expressed as a function of site characteristics, as in Eq. (2.18), was also tested empirically for both net household density and net employment density. The specific site characteristics selected were chosen on the basis of the regression results for land use gross density, to be presented later in this chapter; detailed discussion of most of the variables will therefore be deferred. The following regression equation was estimated for net residential density:[6]

$$N_R = 3.93 + .04E + .01A - .15M - 9.16Y$$
$$(2.32) \quad (4.76) \quad (3.22) \quad (-2.04) \quad (-2.70)$$
$$[\ .32] \quad [\ .58] \quad [-\ .25] \quad [-\ .42]$$
$$R^2 = .81, \tag{4.4}$$

where E = gross employment density within the community; A = accessibility to employment in other communities; M = minimum zoned residential lot size (in square feet); and Y = fraction of households with incomes over $10,000. The figures in parentheses below the regression coefficients are the t-statistics. The figures in brackets are the elasticities calculated at the point of means; we shall refer to these in Section III of this

---

[6] This equation was estimated by two-stage least squares, because one of the site characteristics included in the regression, employment density, is an endogenous variable in the model.

II. Preliminary tests of the model

chapter. As in Eq. (4.3), the income variable was included to standardize somewhat for the extreme heterogeneity of incomes and tastes included in the aggregation of all households.

All of the independent variables are significant at the 99 percent confidence level. None of the other site characteristics in the model added significantly to the explanatory power of this regression. This is consistent with the results of the gross residential density regressions to be presented in Section III. As we shall see, the other site characteristics significantly affect the gross density of only a small subset of households, those in the upper income classes.

This regression is very interesting in that it provides striking substantiation of one of the corollaries of Alonso's location model, cited in Chapter 1. That model concludes that the quantity of land demanded by each household—that is, net residential density—can be expressed as a function of the site's accessibility to economic activity and the household's preferences for space, which Alonso feels will depend primarily upon income.[7] Moreover, he recognizes that minimum lot zoning restrictions may force net density below the free market equilibrium.[8] The signs of the regression coefficients in Eq. (4.4) are precisely those predicted by the Alonso model.

Several regressions were estimated in an attempt to explain net density of total employment in a similar fashion, using site characteristics of the model. Unfortunately, none of the regressions yielded reasonable, significant coefficients. This inability to explain net employment density is not surprising. Total employment is a gross aggregation of industries with a wide variety of production functions; the theory upon which Eq. (2.18) was based assumed a single industry with a single production function. In the case of residential net density, we were able to circumvent the problem of heterogeneity by standardiz-

---

[7] Alonso, *Location and Land Use*, pp. 106–109.
[8] *Ibid.*, pp. 118–123.

ing for income; there is no comparable variable that can be used to standardize for the heterogeneity of industries included in total employment.

Equation (4.4) demonstrates empirically that net residential density can be explained as a function of site characteristics alone, without reference to the price of land. The theory further implies that once these site characteristics are given, the value of land in a particular use is uniquely determined. Thus, given site characteristics and land use, the price of land should have no independent effect upon net density. Since this theoretical proposition will be important in the interpretation of the gross density regressions, it will be useful to test it empirically by adding the average value of land, P, to regression Eq. (4.4). The resulting parameter estimates are

$$N_R = 4.11 + .04P + .03E + 0.1A - .14M - 9.93Y$$
$$(2.29) \quad (.50) \quad (2.57) \quad (2.34) \quad (-1.78) \quad (-2.58)$$
$$R^2 = .80. \tag{4.5}$$

The estimated coefficient of P is virtually zero; this supports the theoretical conclusion. In the estimation of gross residential densities by income class, then, we can be confident that the price of land is serving only as a proxy for competing bids from other land uses and affects only areal shares.

III. Estimation of land use gross densities: residential land uses

In Chapter 3, a total of eleven site characteristics that may be expected to influence residential land use were defined: employment opportunities inside the community; employment opportunities in neighboring communities; measures of quality of six municipal services (education, streets and highways, parks and recreation, water and sewers, fire and police protection);

III. Land use gross densities: residential land uses 69

the condition of the housing stock; minimum residential lot sizes; and the equalized property tax rate. Two measures of competing bids from other land uses were also defined: the price of land and residential rents. The results of two-stage least squares regression of the five income classes of residential gross density upon this set of thirteen variables are summarized in Table 4.2.[9] Also included in Table 4.2 is the regression of median gross rent per room upon a subset of these variables; it will be recalled that residential rents were introduced as an endogenous variable of the model, to be determined simultaneously with the land use densities.

The entries in Table 4.2, rather than being actual regression coefficients, are estimated elasticities of the dependent variable with respect to the independent variable, calculated at the point of means. The t-statistic for the regression coefficient is presented in parentheses below the elasticity. Elasticities were preferred to regression coefficients because they facilitate comparison of the different regressions by standardizing for the units of the dependent variable. The elasticities are calculated at the point of means because the elasticity with respect to a given variable varies continuously over a linear regression plane.

In general, the regression equations of Table 4.2 provide fairly good explanations of the dependent variables, as judged by the multiple correlation coefficient, R^2 (see line 15, Table 4.2). Except for the highest income class, each of the regression equations explains about 70 percent of the variance of the dependent variable.[10] The expression "n.s." in the table indicates

[9] The regressions in Table 4.2 and the gross employment density regressions in Section IV of this chapter were estimated as a single simultaneous system, using two-stage least squares. They are presented separately for clarity of exposition only.

[10] The lower explanatory power of the highest income class regression may result from several factors. For one thing, this class is much smaller than the other classes (see line 16, Table 4.2: "Mean of Dependent Variable"), so that unexplained variations that are very small in terms of number of households will represent relatively large

TABLE 4.2

Estimated elasticities at point of means

Independent variables	Gross household density by income class					Median gross rent per room
	Over $25,000	$10,000–$24,999	$6000–$9999	$3000–$5999	Under $3000	
Constant	−.07	.98	2.83	3.20	.82	12.71
	(−.52)	(2.38)	(2.31)	(2.11)	(1.44)	(17.29)
Accessibility to employment	1.06	.44	.72	.95	.66	.14
	(2.21)	(2.04)	(2.58)	(2.31)	(1.42)	(4.25)
Employment density	n.s.[a]	.27	.27	.47	.64	n.s.[a]
		(1.65)	(4.04)	(4.82)	(5.90)	
Minimum zoned lot size	.50	−.38	−.25	−.24	−.27	
	(1.74)	(−2.43)	(−1.99)	(−1.30)	(−1.34)	
Median gross rent per room			−1.59	−2.66	−1.92	
			(−1.53)	(−1.74)	(−1.12)	
Parks and recreation expenditure per acre	n.s.[a]	.55	n.s.[a]	n.s.[a]	n.s.[a]	n.s.[a]
		(1.59)				

Educational expenditure per pupil	.16 (3.13)	.05 (1.66)	n.s.[a]	n.s.[a]	n.s.[a]	.01 (1.40)
Housing condition index	-.31 (1.02)	n.s.[a]				-.06 (-2.08)
Equalized property tax rate	n.s.[a]	-.44 (-1.48)				.03 (.83)
Average price of land	n.s.[a]	-.78 (-1.30)				.05 (2.21)
Lack of municipal water and/or sewers	n.s.[a]	n.s.[a]				.02 (3.66)
Burglary insurance	n.s.[a]	n.s.[a]	n.s.[a]	n.s.[a]	n.s.[a]	n.s.[a]
Highway expenditure per acre	n.s.[a]	n.s.[a]	n.s.[a]	n.s.[a]	n.s.[a]	n.s.[a]
Fire insurance	n.s.[a]	n.s.[a]	n.s.[a]	n.s.[a]	n.s.[a]	n.s.[a]
R^2	.52	.68	.73	.70	.73	.80
Mean of dependent variable	.10	.76	1.53	1.29	.43	15.83
Standard error of estimate	.10	.29	.55	.68	.25	.97

Note: Figures in parentheses are t-statistics.
[a] Did not add significantly to explanatory power of regression equation.

that the independent variable did not add significantly to the explanatory power of the equation; the criteria of significance used in excluding these variables were the t-statistics of the regression coefficient and the F-statistic for the entire regression. Variables were excluded if the t-statistic was less than 1.0, or if the t-statistic was only slightly greater than 1.0 and addition of the variable lowered the F-statistic. Blank cells in Table 4.2 indicate that the independent variable was deemed inappropriate, a priori, in that regression.

An extremely encouraging aspect of the residential regression results is that every elasticity has the sign predicted by the theoretical considerations of Chapters 2 and 3, and most have reasonable magnitudes. Thus, the basic theory is consistent with the regression results.

The residential density regression results are discussed in the following sections, one independent variable at a time. Then the regression equation for residential rents is considered.

Employment opportunities

Both of the measures of employment opportunities, gross employment density within the community and accessibility to employment in other communities, enter at high levels of significance in nearly all the residential gross density regressions. Moreover, the elasticities vary from one income group to another in approximately the manner predicted by location theory. The Alonso model, for example, predicts that low-income households will be much more closely tied to employment

---

deviations from the mean. Moreover, this income class, being open-ended, is probably much more heterogeneous in terms of income and tastes than any of the others. Finally, it might be argued that such well-to-do households are less constrained by the economic considerations represented by many of the variables in this model and more oriented to social and cultural factors not represented in the model. Indeed, the general lack of significance of the employment and site cost variables in this equation tend to support this reasoning.

III. Land use gross densities: residential land uses

opportunities than high-income households.[11] John Kain has advanced the same hypothesis in his work in urban residential location.[12] Finally, Ira Lowry has presented empirical evidence to substantiate the proposition that low-income workers tend to live closer to their places of work.[13]

The elasticities with respect to employment density within the community do indeed bear out this expectation; the influence of employment density increases monotonically in moving from the higher to the lower income classes. The other employment variable, accessibility to employment in other communities, presents a mixed pattern. There are probably several reasons for this. One is that although employment opportunities in general are probably a stronger influence on lower-income residence than on higher-income residence, one also expects employment *within* the community to become relatively more important than employment outside the community for the lower income classes. If employment within the community becomes markedly more important than accessibility to employment in other communities only for the lowest income class, we would expect the elasticity of residential density to rise as we move to successively lower income groups and then to fall in the lowest income class. This is the pattern observed for the accessibility variable in Table 4.2, with the exception of the highest income class.

The unexpectedly high elasticity in this class probably reflects more than merely employment opportunities. As already mentioned, this residential class is probably sensitive to a number of social and cultural amenities not included in the model; the accessibility index may well be acting as a proxy for some of these amenities, especially the cultural activities of the central

---

[11] Alonso, *Location and Land Use*, pp. 106–109.

[12] John F. Kain, "Journey-to-Work as a Determinant of Residential Location," *Regional Science Association Proceedings* 9(1962): 137–160.

[13] Ira S. Lowry, "Location Parameters in the Pittsburgh Model," *Regional Science Association Proceedings* 10(1963): 145–165.

city. Another possible explanation of this strong accessibility influence is the hypothesis that the strong demand for space normally associated with high income may be offset by demographic factors in this group. If these very high-income households tend to be older people with few dependents, they will place a lower premium on the spaciousness of suburban living and tend to reside nearer the urban core.

Minimum zoned lot size

In Chapter 2 we saw that minimum lot zoning could have any one of several different effects upon residential gross density by income class.[14] First, such regulations may change net density of development without affecting occupancy; this would be the case if the lot size requirement were simply not stringent enough to affect occupancy or if the less dense type of development were the equilibrium land use even in the absence of zoning. Second, the regulation may systematically discriminate against the denser type of residential development that would occur in its absence, with or without changing equilibrium net density in the less dense type of use. Finally, minimum lot requirements may have no effect at all upon gross residential density if they are set at levels below the free market equilibrium lot size.

The regression estimates in Table 4.2 indicate that if density zoning has any systematic effect on occupancy at all, it operates only to the advantage of very high-income households (incomes above $25,000) at the expense of all other income classes. Any marked discriminatory effect between income classes should be manifested in markedly differing elasticities with respect to minimum lot size; the only significant difference among the zoning elasticities in Table 4.2 is the sharp break between the negative elasticities in the four income classes below $25,000 and the positive elasticity in the income class above $25,000.

[14] See Chapter 2, pp. 35–39.

III. Land use gross densities: residential land uses 75

This conclusion runs counter to widely accepted notions about the effect of density zoning. It is commonly assumed that these regulations act as an effective barrier to low-income residential development. The basis for this belief is undoubtedly the strong positive association commonly observed between the stringency of density zoning and the income level of the community. But to conclude that density zoning is responsible for the type of development observed is a post hoc fallacy. We have seen that even very stringent zoning regulations will not affect occupancy if the free market equilibrium land use is the less dense (higher-income) type of development.[15] In most suburban communities (where stringent density zoning is most common), this is undoubtedly the case; our results indicate that it is generally the case in those communities with stringent lot size requirements in this sample region. If this analysis is correct, it is not only true that minimum lot zoning in these communities *does not* affect equilibrium land use; it is the case that it *cannot* affect equilibrium land use because the less dense land uses are optimal in these communities even in the absence of zoning.

It is useful to analyze the estimated elasticities of residential gross densities with respect to the zoning variable in terms of the separate effects of density zoning upon net densities and areal shares of the different income classes. Since gross density is the product of net density and areal share, the elasticity of gross density with respect to the zoning variable can be expressed as simply the sum of the minimum lot size elasticities of net density and areal share.[16]

In Section II of this chapter [Eq. (4.4)], the minimum lot

---

[15] Chapter 2, p. 37.

[16] If for a particular land use we denote net density by N, areal share by A, and the zoning variable by M, the elasticity of gross density with respect to M is

$$\varepsilon_{NA,M} = [d(NA)/dM]M/NA$$
$$= (AdN/dM + NdA/dM)M/NA \qquad (4.6)$$
$$= \varepsilon_{N,M} + \varepsilon_{A,M}.$$

size elasticity of residential net density was estimated to be −.25. Although this value was estimated for total residence, rather than for specific income classes, an income variable was included in the regression to standardize for variations in the socioeconomic level of households in the community. If we can assume that the minimum lot size elasticity of net density is constant over all income classes, then this value provides an estimate of that elasticity. The fact that none of the gross density elasticities for income classes below $25,000 in Table 4.2 differ significantly from −.25, the net density elasticity, indicates that the areal share elasticity is not significantly different from zero for these income classes. Thus, for these income classes, virtually the entire effect of lot size zoning is upon net density rather than upon areal share, that is, rather than upon occupancy.

On the other hand, the minimum lot size elasticity of the areal share devoted to households over $25,000 is large, positive, and very significant; taking $\varepsilon_{N,M}$ to be −.25, we can compute the value of $\varepsilon_{A,M}$ to be .75. This result raises two questions. First, how is it possible for density zoning to enlarge the areal share of this income class so greatly if the areal share of lower income classes is not significantly affected? The answer is that this income class constitutes only a minute fraction of all households; its mean gross density is only .10 as compared to a mean gross density of 4.12 for all households. Thus, even a negligible amount of discrimination against households below the $25,000 income level can produce a marked effect upon the areal share of households above that level.

Second, why does a "threshold" requirement like minimum lot size uniformly affect the net density of all income classes within so broad a range as that represented by the four income classes below $25,000? There are several reasonable explanations for this. It may be, for example, that zoning authorities tend to look to the free market as a standard, simply setting the minimum lot requirement a little larger than that which would be the free market pattern of development; it is certainly plausible that political pressures make zoning authori-

III. Land use gross densities: residential land uses

ties loath to interfere too radically with the market. Such a policy would have little or no effect upon occupancy, resulting simply in reduced net density in the optimal land use; this is precisely the result observed in Eq. (4.4) and Table 4.2.

In pursuing this policy, zoning authorities can allow for the coexistence of several classes of residence in the community by creating several zones with different lot size requirements. If the different classes of residence would be spatially segregated under free market conditions—and casual observation would indicate that this is the normal case—density zones can be defined so as to conform to existing residential patterns and the different lot size minima can be set so as to reduce net density in each class without affecting occupancy in any zone. In the sample region analyzed here, nearly all of the communities that practice density zoning do specify several (usually four or five) different residential zones. Inspection of the different lot requirements within each community indicates that the *minimum minimorum* used here is probably a very good proxy for the entire structure of lot size requirements. Moreover, inspection of zoning maps for several of the communities shows that a single density zone often consists of several separate, irregularly shaped areas; this tends to suggest that density zones are defined so as to conform to existing development patterns.

In summary, then, the regression results with respect to density zoning may be interpreted as indicating only a marginal interference by the zoning authorities in the free market. Lot size requirements seem to be set just below the free market equilibrium for the optimal type of residential development. The existence of spatial segregation of income classes probably allows the zoning authority to affect the net density of each class of housing by establishing separate zones.

Median gross rent per room

The residential rent variable was included in the gross density regressions for the three lower income classes as a measure of competing bids for housing. It is assumed that for these income classes the competing bids for land, as measured by average land values, will affect gross densities via their influence upon residential rents; the price of land is, therefore, not explicitly entered as an explanatory variable in this regression. Similarly, it is assumed that property tax differentials will only affect gross residential densities in these income classes if they are shifted to tenants in the form of rent differentials; the property tax rate was, therefore, excluded from these three regressions as well.

The effect of these variables on gross density can be calculated, however, as the product of the elasticity of residential rents with respect to the independent variable in question and the elasticity of gross density with respect to residential rents.[17] The role of these variables in the determination of residential rents will be discussed in greater detail near the end of this section, when we take up the rent regression in Table 4.2.

The estimated elasticities of gross density with respect to rent levels conform quite well to theoretical expectations. In all three regressions, rents have a strong, fairly significant effect upon gross residential density; the elasticities range from -1.59 to -2.66. One might have expected, a priori, that the effect of rents would be strongest in the lowest income group, rather than the $3000–$5999 class as indicated by these results. The observed pattern may result, however, from a number of factors. Households in the lowest income class are probably much less mobile, and thus less able to take advantage of rent differentials; this will be the case for aged couples, households headed by females, and other family groups typical of this income level. Moreover, this group may have relatively less knowledge of the

[17] For example, if we denote the price of land by P, rent by R, and gross density in a particular use by D, the elasticity of gross density with respect to land values may be written in this fashion:

$$\begin{aligned}\varepsilon_{D,P} &= (dD/dP)(P/D) \\ &= (dD/dR)(dR/dP)(P/R)(R/D) \\ &= (\varepsilon_{D,R})(\varepsilon_{R,P}).\end{aligned} \quad (4.7)$$

III. Land use gross densities: residential land uses

current housing market. In any case, the standard error of estimation of the regression coefficient is large enough to make confident comparisons of the elasticities difficult.

Housing conditions

Apart from the effect of housing conditions upon rent levels, the external diseconomies associated with dilapidated and deteriorating housing turned out to be a rather insignificant factor in residential location. Of the two upper income regressions in which the housing index (percent of dwelling units dilapidated or deteriorating) was included as an explanatory variable, it was totally insignificant in one and significant at only a relatively low level of confidence (about the 85 percent level) in the second, households with incomes over $25,000. The estimated elasticity does have the expected negative sign in that equation, however.[18]

As explained in Chapter 3, it was deemed inappropriate to include this variable as a measure of amenities in the regressions for the income classes below $10,000. The partial correlation that emerges if the housing index is included in those regressions is positive, because poor quality housing is, typically, inexpensive housing and, therefore, attracts households in these income classes. We can use the elasticity relationship of Eq. (4.7) to estimate the strength of this effect.[19] The elasticity of

---

[18] This negative partial correlation is *not* simply a reflection of the fact that high-income residents themselves live in nice homes. The gross density of residence in this income class is virtually uncorrelated with the housing condition index; the zero-order correlation between the two is .06. This lack of correlation might be expected from the fact that households in this income class occupy far too small a fraction of all dwelling units (less than 5 percent) to materially affect the percentage of dwelling units that are dilapidated or deteriorating.

[19] Unfortunately, there is no test of significance for the derived elasticity, because we have no measure of the covariance of the regression coefficients involved.

rent levels with respect to the housing index is −.06; this implies housing condition elasticities of .10, .16, and .12, respectively, for residential gross densities in the income classes $6000–$9999, $3000–$5999, and less than $3000.

Property tax rates

As noted earlier, the property tax variable was included as an explanatory variable in only the two upper income regressions because it was assumed that its effect on residential densities in the other income classes would depend upon whether tax differentials are shifted to the tenant in the form of rent differentials. The regression equation for residential rents indicates that there is no significant shifting of property tax differentials and, thus, no tax effect on gross densities in these income classes. This result will be analyzed later in the context of the determination of residential rents.

The tax variable has a fairly strong negative effect upon gross density in the $10,000–$24,999 income class but no significant effect upon gross household density in the income range above $25,000. The latter result conforms with the general lack of significance of purely economic variables in this income range.

The negative partial correlation between property tax rates and gross residential density in the $10,000–$24,999 income class merits further analysis. As we have already noted, there may be a problem of interpretation involved here. Property tax rates have been assumed to be exogenously determined; if, in fact, tax rates are influenced by the endogenous variables of the model, the direction of causation in such a correlation may run from land use density to tax rate level, rather than vice versa.

For example, it might be argued that greater density of high-income residential development implies a larger per capita tax base, which allows lower tax rates for a given level of municipal service expenditures per capita. In actuality, this does not appear to be the case. Gross residential density in this in-

III. Land use gross densities: residential land uses

come class is virtually uncorrelated with property tax rates and tax base; the zero-order correlation between this gross density and tax rates is .13, and its zero-order correlation between this equalized per capita tax base is $-.16$. Moreover, in an effort to test this hypothesis further, several regression equations were estimated expressing the property tax rate as a function of variables of the model, chiefly the service quality variables and land use gross densities. In no case was a multiple correlation coefficient significantly different from zero obtained.

It appears, therefore, that we are justified in taking tax rates as exogenously determined and the direction of causation as running from tax rates to land use density. For households in the $10,000–$24,999 income class, then, property tax differentials do appear to reduce gross residential density in the manner predicted by the theoretical analysis.

Land values

The average price per acre of land in the community was introduced in the two highest income class regressions as a measure of competing bids for land. In the $10,000–$24,999 income range, the estimated coefficient has the expected negative sign, indicating that the areal share of this residential class varies inversely with the productivity of other land uses, ceteris paribus; the regression coefficient is significant at the 90 percent confidence level. The coefficient of the land value variable in the highest income class regression was not significantly different from zero at an acceptable confidence level. The effect of competing bids from nonresidential uses upon the gross densities of households with incomes below $10,000, although not explicitly estimated in these regressions, can be calculated from the effect of the land value variable upon residential rents. As shown in Eq. (4.7), the elasticity of gross density with respect to land values is simply the product of the elasticity of gross density with respect to rent and the elasticity of rent with respect to land values. The derived elasticities of gross density with respect to the price of land are −.08, −.13, and −.10, respectively, for the income classes $6000–$9999, $3000–$5999, and less than $3000.

Expenditure on education and on parks and recreation

Significant partial correlation coefficients were estimated for these two municipal service variables only in the two income classes above $10,000. Expenditure on parks and recreation per developed acre was significant in the $10,000–$24,999 class, and educational expenditure per pupil, expressed as deviation from the Massachusetts average, was significant in both income classes over $10,000.[20] All three elasticities are positive, as one would expect.[21] Each of these variables was introduced into the gross density regressions for the other three income classes; neither yielded significant coefficients in any of those three regressions.[22]

---

[20] The second measure of educational quality proposed in Chapter 3, the pupil–teacher ratio, was also used as an explanatory variable in these regressions in place of expenditure per pupil. The parameters estimated for this variable were broadly similar to those of the expenditure variable, but at generally lower levels of significance.

[21] The comparatively small elasticity of high-income gross residential density with respect to educational expenditure per pupil is in part merely a reflection of the way this variable is defined. As noted above, the variable used is the deviation from the state average; this variable has a very small mean, giving rise to lower elasticities than would have resulted had we used, say, the absolute level of expenditure per pupil. The significance of the coefficient and the other parameters of the equation are, of course, invariant with respect to such linear transformations.

[22] It may seem asymmetrical to include these two variables in both the rent regression and the three lower income density regressions while excluding the tax rate, land value, and sewer and water variables from those gross density regressions on the grounds that they were included in the rent regression. There is a fundamental difference between these two sets of variables, however. The latter three

III. Land use gross densities: residential land uses

Unfortunately, these three significant regression coefficients are very difficult to interpret because the direction of causation is ambiguous. If the gross density of high-income households acts as a proxy for the fraction of voters in these income classes, it may be that the positive correlation obtained here reflects the fact that these households exert political pressure to obtain high quality services. In that event, the direction of causation may run from gross residential density in these income classes to quality of service, rather than vice versa. Indeed, there are strong simple correlations between each of these residence classes and these two service quality variables, ranging from .53 to .74.

In an attempt to clarify the situation, several regression equations were estimated, explaining these service levels as a function of a set of independent variables, including the two residential gross densities. The rationale was that if we could explain the service level variable with variables that are uncorrelated with the gross densities and if the gross density measures did not enter significantly in these regressions, then we could legitimately assume that the service variables are exogenously determined. Educational expenditure per pupil was regressed upon the property tax base per pupil, the property tax rate, median income in the community, the percentage of pupils attending private schools, median years of education completed by persons over twenty-four, and (in separate regressions) the two residential gross densities.[23] Expenditure on parks per developed acre was regressed upon the tax rate, tax base per developed acre, median family income, and gross residential density in the $10,000–$24,999 class.

---

variables all represent site costs that will affect the renter only if they are passed on to him in the form of higher rents; the former two are municipal services that he enjoys regardless of whether they are capitalized into rent levels.

[23] Rather surprisingly, all of the first four variables are only weakly correlated with the gross density variables; all of the zero-order correlations are less than .40 and most of them are less than .20.

In both cases, a highly significant, positive partial correlation remained between the quality of service and the high-income gross density variables. The results, therefore, were inconclusive; a more refined test of direction of causation is obviously required. One possible solution might be to bring these two variables into the model as endogenous variables and thus, in the estimation procedure, "purge" them of the influence of the other endogenous variables of the model. This approach was originally contemplated but it was decided that such an extension of the model was beyond the scope of this study. To properly account for these service levels, one would have to construct a theory of the supply and demand for municipal services; such a theory is practically nonexistent in the literature.

In spite of the unresolved problem of causation, the regression results for these two services do yield important and useful information. One certainly expects to find a two-way interaction between service levels and household income levels, with high quality services attracting high-income households and these households in turn demanding high quality services. The regression results tend to confirm this expectation. Moreover, either one of the interpretations implies a significant concern for these services in the income classes above $10,000. Given this concern, it is highly probable that public education and parks and recreation are given at least some consideration in the location decisions of high-income households. On the other hand, these service variables seem to have no significant effect at all on households in the income range below $10,000. Finally, it was important to include these variables because, as noted in Chapter 3, it is necessary to standardize for municipal service quality if we are to obtain a legitimate measure of the influence of tax rates on residential location.

Expenditures for police and fire protection,
water and sewers, and highways

The quality variables for these municipal services were uniformly insignificant in the regression equations for residential

III. Land use gross densities: residential land uses 85

gross densities. Any one of several explanations may account for this. It may be, of course, that these services are not important considerations in the residential location decision or that their quality does not vary sufficiently within our sample for intercommunity differentials to have any significant effect. It may also be that the variables used here are not appropriate quantifications of service quality.

Inspection of the data reveals a fairly convincing explanation for the lack of significance of at least one of the quality variables, fire insurance premiums. Although there are seven premium classifications for Massachusetts cities and towns, within the sample of communities used here only three different premium rates are represented, and these range only from $33 to $39 per year for a $20,000 home. This differential of $6 per year could hardly be expected to affect residential location significantly.[24]

The dummy variable for lack of municipal provision of water supply or sewage disposal was included in only the two upper income regressions because this variable was included as a determinant of residential rents, which measure site costs in the other three regressions. Although this variable was insignificant in those two gross density regressions, it does have a highly significant effect upon rents and, therefore, affects gross

---

[24] An interesting fact emerges from the inspection of fire insurance premiums, however. The next rate classification above those represented in the sample carries a premium of $67 per annum, an increase of $28. This suggests that municipal policy within an urbanized area such as this is to provide fire protection that falls within a fairly narrow range of generally accepted quality standards. This conclusion is strengthened by the fact that per capita expenditures for fire protection vary much more widely within the sample than does quality of fire protection, as measured by insurance premiums. The coefficient of variation (ratio of standard deviation to mean) for per capita expenditures on fire protection was 3.53, as compared to a coefficient of variation of .01 for the quality variable. It appears that, for this service at least, quality standards are fairly uniform and local governments spend whatever is required to provide the generally accepted level of protection.

densities in the lower income classes to some extent. As might be expected, its effect upon rents is small (elasticity of .02); the derived elasticities of gross density with respect to this variable are −.03, −.05, and −.04, respectively, for the income classes $6000–$9999, $3000–$5999, and less than $3000.

The determinants of median gross rent per room

The regression results for residential rents, presented in Table 4.2, indicate that rents are significantly affected by the level of land values, the provision of municipal water and sewers, accessibility, housing conditions, and educational expenditure per pupil.

The introduction of the following variables did not add significantly to the explanatory power of the regression: gross employment density within the community, expenditures on parks and recreation per developed acre, insurance premiums for burglary and fire, expenditures on highways per developed acre, and median family income in the community.

The insignificance of several of these variables is somewhat surprising. One might have expected, for example, that employment opportunities within the community would have at least as great an effect on rents as accessibility to employment in other communities. It may well be, however, that the advantages of proximity to employment opportunities within the community are offset by external diseconomies created by industry. Many types of industrial activity decrease the amenity value of residential property nearby by producing traffic congestion, noise, air pollution, generally unsightly buildings, and other nuisances.

Another of these variables that might have been expected to significantly affect rents is median family income. Its insignificance is rather difficult to account for, but there are at least two possible explanations. It may be that median family income for all families is not a good measure of the income level of

III. Land use gross densities: residential land uses

renter households. It is more likely, however, that by including in the regression most of the variables that are valued differentially by different income classes, we have already incorporated the income effect into the regressions.

The variables that are significant all have the expected signs. The relatively small elasticities estimated for these variables simply reflect the fact that the variance of the rent variable is rather small as compared to its mean; the coefficient of variation for this variable (ratio of standard deviation to mean) is only .12. The significant independent variables explain 80 percent of the variance of rents, as indicated by the R^2.

The regression results throw some light on the question of capitalization of property tax and service differentials, discussed in Chapter 3. Tax differentials seem to be almost entirely capitalized into the value of land and improvements; this is indicated by the insignificance of the tax rate variable, implying no shifting of tax differentials to the tenant. For comparison, we can calculate the tax rate elasticity that would be implied by total shifting of tax differentials. The mean tax rate in our sample is .032 per annum; if we assume that the mean value of rental dwelling units is $16,000 and that the mean number of rooms per dwelling unit is 5.0, the tax rate elasticity implied by full shifting is about .52. The estimated elasticity of .03, then, would imply virtually no tax shifting even if it were significant.

At the same time, there also seems to be at least some capitalization of municipal service benefits in the case of education and the provision of water and sewers. That is, differentials in these variables give rise to rent differentials. The coefficient of the dummy variable for lack of municipal water or sewers indicates that private provision of these services raises monthly rents by about $1.92 per room, or about $120 per year for a five-room house. The regression coefficient of the educational expenditure variable indicates that a $1.00 increase in expenditure per pupil will be accompanied by an increase in monthly rents of about $.006 per room, or about $.36 per year for a five-room house. Unfortunately, there is no way to define full capitalization of these benefits, and, therefore, no way to measure the proportion of these benefits recouped by property owners.

As indicated in Chapter 3, capitalization of municipal service benefits and property tax differentials may be expected if the supply of housing is relatively inelastic or if the demand for housing is relatively elastic with respect to rents.[25] Of course, in a reduced-form expression for residential rents such as this, there is no way of separating out these two elasticities. However, as we noted in the earlier discussion, there are good a priori grounds for expecting both conditions to hold at the community level. The existence of numerous alternative sites in other communities with roughly similar characteristics, together with a relatively mobile population, would lead us to expect a highly elastic demand for housing in any one community. At the same time, the long life and immobility of the housing stock, together with the relatively slow rate of change in the total stock, points to a highly inelastic supply of housing in any given community. The hypothesis of highly elastic demand and highly inelastic supply at the community level is also in agreement with the relatively small variation in residential rents observed in this sample.[26]

A second question posed in Chapter 3 that may be analyzed in the light of these results is the question of whether renovation of dilapidated or deteriorating dwelling units will be profitable to the owner. If the parameters of this rent regression may be taken as applicable to individual dwelling units, the regression coefficient of the housing index measures the differential in monthly gross rent per room attributable to substandard condition. The value of this coefficient is -11.39, indicating that renovation of a five-room dwelling unit would add $684 to the owner's annual rental income. Thus, renovation will be profitable if the total annual capital cost of renovation is less than $684.

[25] See Chapter 3, pp. 54–58.
[26] See Chapter 4, p. 87.

IV. Land use gross densities: employment uses

It is an open question whether renovation can be accomplished at costs of this magnitude. Eugene Smolensky has investigated the feasibility of renovating substandard dwellings at annual costs in the range of $480–$725; his results seem to warrant cautious optimism.[27] In a critique of Smolensky's work, however, Michael Stegman raises some serious questions as to the reliability of Smolensky's data.[28] A definitive answer to this question would seem to await better data on actual renovation costs.

In any case, it should be emphasized that the $684 figure obtained here is probably a generous estimate of the annual returns to renovation of a *single* dwelling unit. The estimated elasticity of rents with respect to community housing conditions undoubtedly incorporates at least some neighborhood effects that could not be recouped by individual property owners unless the entire neighborhood were renovated simultaneously.

IV. Estimation of land use gross densities: employment uses

Regression equations were estimated to explain the gross density of three broad classes of employment: manufacturing; retail trade, including nonprofessional services; and professional and governmental.[29] Together, these three employment categories account for about 79 percent of all employment in the sample region. In addition, regression results are presented in

---

[27] Eugene Smolensky, "Public Housing or Income Supplements: The Economics of Housing for the Poor," *Journal of the American Institute of Planners* 34(March 1968): 94–101.

[28] Michael A. Stegman, "Comment on 'Public Housing or Income Supplements: The Economics of Housing for the Poor'," 34(May 1968): 195–198.

[29] Employment data by place of work for 1963 were furnished by the Massachusetts Department of Public Works; see Appendix for detailed data sources.

this section for the combined class of manufacturing and wholesale employment. Wholesale employment accounts for about 7 percent of total employment in the sample region. Reliable employment data by place of work were not available for the sample communities for any other industrial categories.

Gross density of retail employment

Retail trade was assumed to be a primarily market-oriented activity. Household density and median family income within the community and the accessibility index were therefore included among the independent variables as proxies for accessibility to product markets. Property tax rates were included as a cost variable, and the average price of land was entered as a proxy for competing bids from other land uses. The only municipal service variable that might be expected to be important to retail trade is expenditure on highways per developed acre, which measures the extent and quality of the highway network in the community.

The final variable included in the retail trade regression was a dummy variable, which equals 1.0 for Boston and 0.0 for all other communities. This was an attempt to take into account the unique advantages of the central city as a retail trade center. The rationale for this variable is that there is a wide range of retail sales and service activities that are available only in the central city of a metropolitan area. One metropolitan area simply does not provide a large enough market to support more than one or a few outlets for some products or services with marked economies of scale, and the logical location for a single establishment is in the central city. Many of the cultural and entertainment activities of the central city are of this nature, as are a number of other highly specialized products and services. Moreover, Boston is the principal beneficiary of a well-developed transit system servicing a number of communities near the urban core; this may be expected to have a substantial effect

IV. Land use gross densities: employment uses

upon retail trade in Boston. None of the other variables of the model take public transportation into account.

Regression analysis revealed that only three of the seven independent variables described above add significantly to the explanation of gross retail employment density. These three are gross household density, expenditure on highways per developed acre, and the dummy variable for Boston. This set of three variables, however, explains 89 percent of the variance of the dependent variable. The estimated regression equation is[30]

$$D_{RET} = \begin{array}{cccc} -.27 + & .11 D_R + & .44 H + & 3.38 B \\ (-1.93) & (1.96) & (3.50) & (7.30) \\ & [.41] & [.74] & [.10] \end{array} \quad (4.8)$$

$$R^2 = .89,$$

where D_{RET} = gross retail employment density; D_R = gross residential density (in households per acre); H = highway expenditures per developed acre; and B = dummy variable for Boston.

All three of the regression coefficients of the independent variables are estimated at very high levels of significance, as indicated by the t-statistics (in parentheses), and all three coefficients have the expected positive sign. The magnitudes of the estimated elasticities (in brackets) are also plausible, with the possible exception of the large elasticity with respect to highway expenditures. The strong influence of this variable probably reflects the critical dependence of retail trade upon accessibility to pedestrian and vehicular trade. The highway expenditure variable may be thought of as a proxy for the extent of the network of major traffic arteries in the communities; frontage on such arteries may be expected to be a prime consideration in the location of retail establishments.

---

[30] All of the regression equations of this section were estimated by two-stage least squares as a simultaneous system with the residential gross density regressions of Section III.

The coefficient of the dummy variable for Boston reveals a marked asymmetry between Boston and the other communities of the sample. Retail employment density in Boston is 5.12 employees per developed acre; the coefficient of the dummy variable (3.38) indicates that only about one-third of this employment can be explained on the basis of resident population and highway expenditures, weighted by the regression coefficients for the entire sample of thirty-one communities. The other two-thirds is attributable to the central city's unique advantages as a major retail shopping center. It is interesting to note that this asymmetry did not appear in the regression results for all types of employment; neither manufacturing gross density nor gross density of manufacturing and wholesaling combined were significantly affected by the dummy variable for Boston.

It is also of interest to discuss some possible reasons for the insignificance of some of the other variables that were initially introduced to explain retail employment density. For example, it is somewhat surprising at first glance that competing bids from other land uses, as represented by average land values, had no significant effect upon retail density. But if it is true that retail firms place a great premium on sites fronting on major traffic arteries, then it may be that these sites are so much more valuable in retail use than in other uses that even large variations in competing bids will not affect occupancy; that is, this type of site is highly specialized to retail activities.

The insignificance of the tax rate variable may also be plausibly explained. Being closely tied to product markets, the location of retail trade is probably not influenced by cost differentials of the magnitude represented by property tax differentials. Moreover, retail establishments serving a primarily local market probably have less difficulty in shifting tax differentials forward to consumers than, say, a manufacturing firm competing in a regional or a national market.

Median family income might have been expected to influence retail employment density, insofar as it is a measure of

IV. Land use gross densities: employment uses

purchasing power in the community. Its insignificance in the regression may reflect several factors. First, although higher-income households undoubtedly spend more on retail goods and services, their shopping trips are probably dispersed over a wider area, so that local retail trade does not benefit proportionally from their expenditures; at least one study of shopping habits in the Boston area confirms this hypothesis.[31] Second, if retail establishments in high-income communities systematically sell more expensive goods and services, retail employment may not be proportional to sales.

Gross density of professional and governmental employment

The use of professional and governmental employment, a rather heterogeneous category, was dictated by considerations of data availability; this was the only well-defined class of employment other than retail, manufacturing, and wholesale for which data were available for all the communities of the sample region.

Professional employment may be expected to exhibit most of the same locational characteristics as retail trade, in that it is primarily a market-oriented industry. We may expect that Boston is the site of a good deal of professional employment that probably can be explained only on the grounds that Boston is the center of the metropolitan, and even the New England, area. In particular, highly centralized activities, such as communications media and finance and their supporting professional services, major medical centers, and law firms may be expected to locate in Boston.

As a first approximation, government employment can also

---

[31] John P. Alevizos and Allen E. Beckwith, *Downtown and Suburban Shopping Habits of Greater Boston,* Boston University College of Business Administration (Boston: Boston Herald and Traveler, 1954): Table 8, p. 18.

be considered to be "market-oriented"; here the "market" is simply population, which may be appropriately measured by gross household density in the community. Again, we expect a disproportionate share of this type of employment to locate in Boston because it is the state capital and the regional headquarters for a number of federal governmental activities, so that inclusion of the dummy variable for Boston is again indicated.

With these considerations in mind, the same set of seven site characteristics that were tested in the retail employment equation were initially included in the gross density regression for professional and governmental employment. Of these seven, it was found that two significant variables, household density and the Boston dummy, account for 53 percent of the variance of the dependent variable; the estimated parameters are

$$D_{PG} = \begin{array}{c} -.54 \\ (-1.24) \end{array} + \begin{array}{c} .39D_R \\ (4.36) \\ [1.36] \end{array} + \begin{array}{c} 2.44B \\ (1.91) \\ [\ .07] \end{array} \quad (4.9)$$

$$R^2 = .53.$$

These results conform quite well to the parameters estimated for retail employment, although the explanatory power of the regression is much lower, probably owing to the heterogeneity of activities included in this class of employment. Both regression coefficients have the expected sign and both are significant at high levels of confidence. As might be expected, the results indicate that this type of activity simply follows population, with the exception of the large concentration in Boston. The gross density of professional and governmental employment in Boston is 5.58; the coefficient of the Boston dummy indicates that about 44 percent of this employment density is attributable to Boston's unique role as a regional center of professional and governmental activity.

The insignificance of the other independent variables initially included can be rationalized along the same lines as the

IV. Land use gross densities: employment uses

arguments advanced with respect to retail employment, at least for professional employment. The insignificance of the highway variable, which figures prominently in retail location, probably reflects the lesser dependence of professional activities upon proximity to pedestrian and vehicular traffic and the fact that governmental activities are relatively independent of this kind of consideration.

Gross density of manufacturing employment

Manufacturing activity may be assumed to be less closely tied to product markets than retail trade or professional employment. We expect, a priori, that site costs will be more important determinants of location for manufacturing. Two cost variables were entered as independent variables in this regression: the property tax rate and the dummy variable for lack of municipal water supply or sewage disposal. Average land values were entered as a measure of competing bids for land, and gross household density and the accessibility index were introduced as measures of accessibility to labor supplies. The rationale underlying the latter two variables is that the larger the labor supply a firm has to draw upon, the better are its chances of obtaining workers with the particular skills it requires. Gross density of retail employment was introduced as a measure both of markets for manufactured products and of supplies of business, financial, and transportation services necessary to manufacturing activity. Finally, the dummy variable for Boston was included to test for the kind of locational asymmetry between Boston and the other sample communities found in the case of retail trade and professional and governmental employment.

Four of these variables were found to be significant at acceptable levels of confidence; the regression results for this set of independent variables are

$$D_{MFG} = 1.68 - .80TX - .18P + .49D_R + 2.94D_{RET}$$
$$(1.45) \quad (-1.84) \quad (-2.40) \quad (1.77) \quad (4.04)$$
$$[-1.32] \quad [-1.24] \quad [1.06] \quad [1.62]$$

$$R^2 = .56, \tag{4.10}$$

where D_{MFG} = gross density of manufacturing employment; TX = equalized property tax rate (in percent); P = average price of land per acre ($\times 10^{-3}$); D_R = gross residential density (in households per acre); and D_{RET} = gross retail employment density.

Virtually identical regression estimates were obtained for gross density of the aggregate class of manufacturing and wholesale employment, D_{MW}, although attempts to estimate gross density of wholesale employment alone failed to produce significant parameters with reasonable elasticities. The regression results for the combined industries are

$$D_{MW} = 1.64 - .79TX - .18P + .50D_R + 2.99D_{RET}$$
$$(1.41) \quad (-1.80) \quad (-2.39) \quad (1.76) \quad (4.05)$$
$$[-1.29] \quad [-1.22] \quad [1.05] \quad [1.62]$$

$$R^2 = .57. \tag{4.11}$$

The failure of the variables in the model to predict density of wholesale employment alone is probably attributable to the fact, mentioned earlier, that wholesale employment is a very small fraction of total employment; unexplained variations that are small in terms of absolute numbers of employees will therefore result in relatively large unexplained variation of the dependent variable. It is interesting to note, however, that the four independent variables explained a slightly larger fraction of the variance of the combined industries' employment than of manufacturing employment alone.

In both cases, all four coefficients are significant at the 95 percent confidence level and have the theoretically expected

IV. Land use gross densities: employment uses

sign. As was anticipated, the cost variables of tax rates and land values exert a stronger locational influence on this industry, as indicated by estimated elasticities of -1.32 and -1.24, respectively. Indeed, manufacturing is the only industry for which we have discovered a strong, significant property tax effect.

This is entirely reasonable, though; unlike the other industries we have considered, manufacturing belongs to the class of industry that E. M. Hoover has termed "foot-loose."[32] That is, manufacturing is not closely tied to product and materials markets because it is an intermediate stage of production dealing with fairly compact, easily transported raw materials and selling its products in sufficient quantities to keep transport costs per unit low. Thus, a manufacturing firm is free to locate anywhere within a wide geographic area, choosing its specific site on the basis of cost differentials such as taxes, labor costs and labor efficiency, land prices, and transport costs.

The regression results support this analysis. Tax rates and land prices exert a strong negative influence, and household density, which we have interpreted as a labor market proxy, has a large, positive elasticity. The very strong, highly significant, positive elasticity with respect to retail density may represent several things. An important consideration that it probably represents, and that is not accounted for by the other variables, is the availability of truck transportation.

The lower explanatory power of this regression, as compared to, say, the retail density equation, may also be due in part to the "foot-loose" nature of manufacturing. If even small cost differentials are important determinants of location, it is difficult to capture all the relevant intercommunity differentials with a manageable set of quantifiable variables; thus, a good deal of locational variation must go unexplained.

The tax influence indicated by the strong negative elasticity of gross manufacturing density with respect to tax rates should

---

[32] Edgar Malone Hoover, *The Location of Economic Activity* (New York: McGraw-Hill, 1948), p. 36.

be analyzed further. As in the case of the significant tax effect found in the $10,000–$24,999 residential class, we must ask whether this simply reflects a tax base effect, with valuable industrial property allowing low tax rates. Again, this does not seem to be the case. The zero-order correlation between gross manufacturing density and property tax rates is positive (.42), rather than negative as the foregoing argument would suggest. Moreover, in the regressions described earlier (page 81) in which property tax rates were estimated as a function of variables of the model, gross manufacturing density was included as an independent variable; in no case did it significantly affect tax rates, even at very low levels of confidence. It seems legitimate, then, to interpret the regression results as indicating a strong property tax effect upon the location of manufacturing activity.

The average price of land

In Chapter 2, an equation was derived expressing average land values as a linear function of land use gross densities.[33] This result, Eq. (2.28), can in principle be tested empirically since all of the variables of the equation are directly observable quantities.

Unfortunately, several very serious technical problems were encountered in attempts to estimate the parameters of Eq. (2.28) empirically. The first problem involves the high degree of collinearity among the land use gross densities. With the exception of the two highest income residential classes, the zero-order correlations between the land use gross densities all fall in the range of .65 to .98. With such high correlation among the explanatory variables, the estimated regression coefficients are extremely unstable and cannot be relied upon with any degree of confidence.

The second major estimation problem involved the limi-

---

[33] See Chapter 2, p. 40.

IV. Land use gross densities: employment uses

tations of the particular computational system used in calculating the two-stage least squares estimates for this study. Estimation of this equation, possibly because it contains so many highly collinear endogenous variables, seems to be subject to serious computational errors due to the rounding off of multiplicative cross-products to a specified number of decimal places. Evidence of such computational inaccuracy is the fact that the R^2 of the regression of land values upon all eight gross density variables was .67, but deletion of two of the independent variables raised the R^2 to .79. Such a result is theoretically impossible; additional variables, even insignificant ones, should never reduce the R^2.[34] The only explanation seems to be that rounding errors are influencing the results.

In an attempt to avoid both the problems of collinearity and of rounding errors, several modified versions of Eq. (2.28) were tested empirically. Aggregate classes of residence and employment were introduced as explanatory variables, in order to reduce the number and collinearity of the independent variables. The principal criteria used in aggregation of the land use classes were the zero-order correlations between the various gross densities; highly correlated activities were summed to form single land use categories. Residential land use categories defined in this manner include households with incomes under $10,000, those with incomes over $10,000, and all households; aggregate employment classes include total retail, professional, and governmental employment, and all employment.

Regression results for four different sets of these variables are presented in Table 4.3. The zero-order correlations among the aggregate classes of employment and among the aggregate classes of residence are still very high (on the order of .85 to .99), so that only one residential land use and one industrial land use are included in each regression to reduce collinearity

---

[34] The R^2 under consideration is *not* adjusted for degrees of freedom.

TABLE 4.3

Estimated elasticities at point of means

Independent variables	Regression number			
	(1)	(2)	(3)	(4)
Constant	−3.13	−3.44	−3.83	−28.87
	(−1.43)	(−1.48)	(−1.48)	(−2.45)
Households under $10,000 (gross density)	n.s.[a]	n.s.[a]		
Households over $10,000 (gross density)	.87	.93	1.03	
	(5.15)	(5.25)	(5.44)	
All households (gross density)				1.01
				(3.22)
Median family income				1.90
				(2.60)
Total employment (gross density)		.33		
		(3.92)		
Retail, professional, and government employment (gross density)	.36			.26
	(4.51)			(1.75)
Manufacturing employment (gross density)			.25	
			(2.93)	
R^2	.77	.75	.68	.62
Standard error of regression	5.80	6.16	6.86	7.66

Note: Figures in parentheses are t-statistics.

[a] This variable did not add significantly to the explanatory power of the regression.

among the independent variables. In the fourth regression, where the residential land use variable includes all households, median family income has been introduced to standardize for socioeconomic heterogeneity.

In general, the regressions provide a relatively good explanation of average land values, especially the first two regressions, which explain about three-fourths of the variance of land values. All but two of the regression coefficients of the land use

IV. Land use gross densities: employment uses

gross densities are significant at the 99 percent confidence level and all have positive signs, as required by Eq. (2.28). Moreover, the regression constants in all except the fourth regression are very close to zero (as compared to the dependent variable, which has a mean value of 13.37), as predicted by the theory. The large negative constant in the fourth equation is due to the inclusion of median family income as an independent variable.

The estimated elasticities of the residential gross density variables are remarkably similar, all falling within the narrow range between .87 and 1.03; similarly, the elasticities of the employment gross density variables fall within the narrow range between .25 and .36. Thus, the choice of aggregate land use classes to be used as explanatory variables does not seem to affect greatly the regression parameters. From the standpoint of explanatory power, however, gross density of high-income households seems to be somewhat superior to total residential density standardized for median family income as a residential variable, and either total employment density or gross density of retail, professional, and governmental employment seems to be preferable to manufacturing employment as an employment variable.[35] Similar regressions were estimated using gross density of households with incomes below $10,000 as the residential variable, but while the estimated coefficients conformed to the same general pattern as those in Table 4.3, the explanatory power of these regressions was markedly lower than that of the regressions in Table 4.3.

The regression results in general, then, substantiate the theoretical formulation of the determinants of average land values contained in Eq. (2.28). Although the regressions of Table 4.3 are not precisely of the form specified by that equation, they seem to be the best formulation of the relation that can be tested empirically.

[35] The similarity of results obtained with total employment density and gross density of retail, professional, and governmental employment reflects the fact that the zero-order correlation between these two variables is .96.

5

Summary of findings and implications for policy

I. The empirical findings

The introductory chapter outlined five central hypotheses that are embodied in the conventional analysis of intraurban location. The empirical findings of this study, while falling short of a definitive test of these hypotheses, can shed a good deal of light upon them. In this section, the relevant findings of this study with respect to each of these hypotheses are summarized.

Hypothesis 1: The residential location of low-income households is more sensitive to employment opportunities and housing costs than that of higher-income households.

The regression results generally support this hypothesis. The estimated elasticity of gross residential density with respect to employment density within the community declines monotonically (from .64 to .27) over the income classes up to $25,000, with no significant effect being evident for households in the income class above $25,000. The pattern of the estimated elasticities with respect to accessibility to employment in other communities is less clear. This elasticity also declines (from .95 to .44) over the income range $3000–$25,000, but is unexpectedly low (.66) for the lowest income class and high (1.06) for the highest income class. The low value for families with less than $3000 income may merely reflect a very restricted commuting radius for these families, while the high value for families above $25,000 may reflect the importance of accessibility to activities other than employment. These two anomalies notwithstanding, the overall pattern of the estimates is one of decreasing sensitivity of residential location to employment opportunities with rising income.

Likewise, low-income households seem to be more sensitive to housing costs. All three residential classes below $10,000 income exhibit a strong elasticity (between -1.59 and -2.66) with respect to rent levels. The gross density of households in the $10,000–$25,000 range shows moderate sensitivity to the costs of home-ownership (elasticities of $-.44$ and $-.78$ with respect to taxes and land values), whereas neither of these variables appears to affect significantly the residential location of households in the highest income class.

Analysis of net residential densities indicates that net density increases with accessibility, as predicted by the theoretical model, and decreases with rising income. Land costs do not significantly affect net density, holding constant other community characteristics. Thus, it appears that the influence of housing costs upon gross density by income class can legitimately be interpreted as an effect on areal shares, rather than a net density effect.

Hypothesis 2: The residential location of high-income families is sensitive to municipal finance variables, such as service quality and tax rates.

The regression results lend some support to this hypothesis,

I. The empirical findings

although certain problems of interpretation arise. The gross residential densities of both income classes above $10,000 are significantly affected by educational expenditures per pupil, and households in the $10,000–$25,000 range show sensitivity to expenditures on parks and recreation and to tax rates. These variables were uniformly insignificant in the regression equations for the three lowest income classes. Measures of the quality of police and fire protection, water and sewers, and streets and highways yielded insignificant coefficients in all of the residential density equations.

The measures of service "quality" employed here are admittedly crude proxies at best. More refined indices of quality might well have yielded more significant results in some of the residential equations. Still, the overall pattern of results lends credence to the hypothesis that these considerations weigh more heavily in the location decisions of high-income families, and that education is the most important municipal service from the standpoint of residential location. In contrast, as noted earlier, the location decisions of low-income households seem to rest on the more purely economic factors of employment opportunities and housing costs. Indeed, there is a slight indication that educational expenditures may actually reduce the gross density of low-income households, through an increase in rent levels. The magnitude of this effect is extremely small, however.

There is, of course, a very real problem of assigning causality in the observed partial correlations between high-income residential densities and municipal service variables. It may well be that high quality services result from concentrations of high-income families, rather than the reverse. However one interprets these results, though, they indicate a concern on the part of these households with the quality of municipal services—particularly education—that may be expected to influence the location decision.

Hypothesis 3: Restrictive density zoning ordinances in suburban communities operate to exclude low-income families.

The empirical estimates of this study cast doubt upon this hypothesis. Comparison of the estimated effect of lot size requirements on gross residential density by income class with the estimated effect on net densities indicates that such requirements have little influence upon the allocation of land among income classes at the municipal level, with the exception of rather marked discrimination in favor of the very small class of households with incomes above $25,000. The principal effect of density zoning seems to be simply a rather uniform reduction of net residential density in all income classes.

We have argued that this may result from a conscious zoning policy of following the free market allocation of land and simply setting maximum zoned residential densities slightly below the free market optimum. Such a policy would be facilitated by the division of the community into zones roughly corresponding to existing homogeneous socioeconomic neighborhoods, with different lot size requirements within the municipalities of the sample region. Whether residential density zones are in fact drawn in this manner is an open question, and one that is beyond the scope of this study. The observed uniform reduction of residential density in all income classes below $25,000 is entirely consistent with such a policy.

Whether or not zoning authorities consciously act to preserve the free market allocation of land, it may be the case that in the suburban communities where it is practiced, minimum lot zoning cannot change residential land use radically, simply because the less dense uses are the free market optimum anyway. The regression results seem to bear out this line of reasoning, since the lot size requirement seems to have no significant influence upon areal shares by income classes (with the exception of households above $25,000), even though the highest-income communities have the most stringent density zoning regulations.

Hypothesis 4: The distribution of employment opportunities in a metropolitan area is sensitive to land and tax costs.

I. The empirical findings

This hypothesis is supported by the empirical evidence only for the category of manufacturing and wholesale employment. The gross density of employment in these activities shows elasticities on the order of −1.3 with respect to both tax rates and land costs. These variables appear to have no significant effect upon the levels of professional, governmental, and retail employment.

This differential effect of site costs among classes of industry is entirely reasonable. Manufacturing is much less closely tied to local product markets than are the retail and service industries. A manufacturing firm therefore has greater freedom to locate anywhere within a wide geographic area, choosing a specific site on the basis of local cost differentials such as taxes, land prices, and labor and transport costs.

Direct evidence of the product market orientation of retail, professional, and governmental employment is provided by the regression results for these activities. Retail employment and professional and governmental employment are strongly influenced by gross residential density and the unique locational advantages of the central city. In addition, retail trade shows a significant sensitivity to local expenditures for streets and highways, interpreted here as a proxy for access to pedestrian and vehicular traffic.

Hypothesis 5: Property taxes levied on rental housing are shifted forward to tenants.

The analysis of residential rents presented here provides no support for this hypothesis. Property tax differentials do not appear to give rise to rent differentials and, therefore, have no locational impact on renter households, which comprise the majority of households with incomes below $10,000 in the sample region. The property tax rate was statistically insignificant in a regression equation that explained 80 percent of the variance of residential rents. Moreover, even had the tax rate coefficient been significant, the estimated elasticity of rents with respect to tax rates was nowhere near the magnitude required for full shifting of tax differentials; for a five-room, $16,000 home, the elasticity implied by full shifting is about .5, compared to the estimated elasticity of .03.

This conclusion contradicts the generally accepted view of property tax incidence; for example, Dick Netzer contends, "In theory, property taxes on improvements . . . can be expected to be shifted forward to . . . occupants of housing."[1] Yet, it must be emphasized that the conventional wisdom with regard to property tax shifting is based almost entirely upon the assumption of uniform tax rates throughout the urban area; when one takes account of the large variations in tax rates within the urban area, it becomes clear that conditions sufficient for substantial capitalization of tax differentials—elastic demand for housing services and inelastic supply of housing services—probably prevail at the municipal level.

II. Implications for public policy

The model developed and tested in this study was not designed to incorporate directly all of the wide range of policy variables that might be employed to influence the distribution of urban residential and economic activities. Indeed, some of the more interesting governmental policies are not empirically testable because they have no existing program analogs. The model does, however, include several important policy variables, and the structural relationships that it contains allow at least tentative inferences about the probable direct and indirect locational effects of other policies.

However, in discussing the policy implications of the results obtained here, one must bear in mind the limitations of both the data and the statistical procedures underlying these results. Although every effort was made to obtain the best possi-

[1] Netzer, *Economics of the Property Tax*, p. 36.

II. Implications for public policy

ble empirical measures of the variables of interest, several of the variables of the model are rather crude proxies for their theoretical counterparts. This is especially true of the municipal service variables; service quality is a difficult concept to quantify. The measures of land values and tax rates are also subject to error, being based in part upon local assessment procedures. In addition, as already noted, there are serious problems in interpreting the direction of causation in some cases, even though the estimation procedure was designed to eliminate the more severe problems of simultaneity. Finally, all of the results are based upon a relatively small sample of communities in a single urban area at one point in time. Only further research in other areas will prove whether these results are typical of American cities. With this caveat in mind, however, it seems useful to examine various areas of public policy in the light of these findings, tentative though they may be.

Housing policies and low-income residential location

Probably no single set of governmental policies has had so pervasive an effect upon the residential distribution of the urban population as the complex of governmental interventions in the housing market. Urban renewal, public housing, rent supplements, mortgage guarantees, and preferential tax treatment of homeowners have all influenced the locational decisions of urban households.[2] The empirical results of this study confirm the potential locational impact of such programs. Households in all but the highest income class were found to respond to housing cost differentials, with the gross density of low-income

---

[2] For example, Muth estimates that federal tax subsidies to homeowners alone have reduced the central-city population by 3 percent and increased the land area devoted to urban use by 17 percent. Muth, *Cities and Housing*, pp. 319–322.

households exhibiting elasticities with respect to rents ranging from −1.6 to −2.7. High-income households also show a significant response to the index of housing conditions. These findings indicate that public intervention in the housing market can have a very significant impact on the spatial distribution of households by income class.

Urban renewal, for example, typically tends to reduce the proportion of low quality, low-rent dwelling units in the central city. This reduction in supply will, in the short run at least, raise the cost of low quality housing in the central city relative to standard quality housing elsewhere. Given the responsiveness of low-income households to rent differentials, this may be expected to foster decentralization of the low-income population. While this may be viewed as a generally desirable outcome, it should be noted that both the low-income families who move and those who stay in the central city are made worse off in the process because the price of a major item of their consumption has increased. A second effect of the reduction in substandard dwellings resulting from urban renewal will be an increase in the number of high-income households in the central city. According to the estimates derived here, a 10 percent reduction in the number of substandard dwellings would result in a 3 percent increase in the number of households with incomes above $25,000.

Attempts to improve the quality of central-city housing through code enforcement programs will have much the same locational effects as outright demolition. Code enforcement, by raising the minimum level of housing quality, increases the cost of minimum quality housing. To the extent such programs are successful, poor families will be induced to relocate, suffering a welfare loss in the process, and high-income families will find the central city more attractive.

Construction of public housing units in the central city will have just the opposite effects. By increasing the supply of low-cost housing, public housing tends to increase the concentration of low-income families in the central city. In fact, given the size

II. Implications for public policy

of the rent subsidy typically involved in public housing,[3] one would expect virtually a one-for-one increase in the low-income population in the short run, unless existing low-cost housing is displaced by the project. At the same time, the rents of private low quality units should fall, in the short run at least. Thus, both public housing tenants and low-income households in private housing are made better off. The response of high-income households to an increase in the stock of public housing is not unambiguously determined by the present analysis. New public housing units are, almost by definition, standard housing; thus, their construction would not affect the housing condition index employed here. However, the concentration of low-income households generated by public housing may have much the same external effects as those associated with substandard housing, resulting in a decrease in the number of high-income households willing to live in the central city.

All of this relates, of course, to public housing built in the central city. Construction of housing projects in the suburbs suggests the possibility of decentralization of the low-income population without reducing their well-being.

Housing programs that subsidize low-income demand without explicit intervention on the supply side may also have significant locational effects. A variety of such schemes, variously characterized as rent supplements, rent certificates, housing allowances, or housing vouchers, have been proposed or enacted into legislation in the recent years.[4] Suppose, for exam-

---

[3] Public housing authorities are required by law to charge rents that are no more than 80 percent of the cost of comparable rental units in the private market.

[4] For discussions of several variants of the rent supplement approach, see Smolensky, *Public Housing or Income Supplements*, 94–101; Edgar O. Olsen, "A Welfare Economic Evaluation of Public Housing," Ph.D. diss., Rice University, 1968; and Frank de Leeuw, Sam H. Leaman, and Helen Blank, "The Design of a Housing Allowance," Urban Institute Working Paper, No. 112-25 (Washington, D. C.: Urban Institute, 1970).

ple, that a program were initiated that paid a specified fraction of a low-income family's rental costs. Such a subsidy would reduce intraurban rent differentials by the same fraction, thereby lowering somewhat the financial barriers that restrict the poor to the oldest, lowest quality areas of the metropolitan housing market. One would expect such a policy to result in decentralization of the low-income population.

A more pronounced locational impact might be achieved with the so-called "housing voucher" or "rent certificate" approach. This policy would grant each family a rent voucher that private landlords could redeem at face value at the local housing voucher authority. The recipient family would pay a specified fraction of its income for the voucher and could use it to purchase housing anywhere in the area. The terms of the subsidy are thus very much like those of the traditional public housing formula, with two important exceptions. First, receipt of the subsidy is not tied to occupancy of a publicly owned dwelling unit. Second, the recipient would be free to supplement the voucher in order to buy housing of greater value than the face value of the voucher. Such a policy would effectively eliminate the intraurban rent differentials facing recipient families, provided that the face value of the voucher is set high enough to purchase housing in a variety of communities. The potential of this policy for inducing decentralization of the poor is obviously much greater than under the "percentage-of-rent" subsidy described earlier, which reduces but does not eliminate rent differentials. Both alternatives would result in welfare gains to the recipients, in contrast to other policies, such as urban renewal and code enforcement, that promote decentralization.

Either type of rent supplement could be conditioned upon the recipients occupying "standard" housing, somehow defined. Such a condition would increase the potential of the policy for promoting decentralization if standard housing is more readily available in the suburbs than in the central city. It must be emphasized, though, that imposition of this condition will result in a smaller welfare gain to those recipients who would have

II. Implications for public policy

purchased substandard housing with an unconditional subsidy. On the other hand, the resulting reduction in demand for substandard housing should, in the short run, lower the cost of substandard housing to nonrecipient households.

In the longer run, one might expect any significant reduction in the rental value of substandard housing to result in a reduction in the supply made available, through either upgrading or demolition of low quality units. The regression estimates presented here indicate that in the existing market (in 1960), a private landlord could increase the annual rent of a five-room dwelling by at most $684 by upgrading it to standard condition. As noted in Chapter 4, it is an open question whether most substandard units could be renovated at an annual cost of this magnitude (and, again, this is probably a generous estimate of the private returns to renovation). A demand subsidy program that significantly altered the relative demands for standard and substandard units might, however, appreciably widen this differential. Thus, conditioning a rent supplement upon occupancy of standard housing could have a substantial impact on renovation and upgrading.

A final area of public housing policy, in which the implications of this study have already been discussed in some detail, is that of residential density zoning. Here the empirical results cast doubt on the widely held belief that density zoning discourages decentralization of the poor. Such ordinances appear, in fact, to have little impact upon areal shares by income class, although they do tend to reduce net residential density. If this is the case, then the desirability of such policies would seem to turn primarily on whether they generate sufficient external benefits, in terms of more aesthetic residential patterns, to compensate individual landowners for reduced land rents. An additional effect of density zoning, little discussed in the literature, is that, to the extent it reduces net residential densities, it increases the amount of land devoted to urban use and enlarges the extent of the urban area. This effect will increase transportation costs for households living on the urban fringe. In any case, though, the distributional consequences of density zoning would seem to be largely concentrated upon the upper-income residents of suburbia, rather than extending to the low-income population of the central city.

Transportation policies and residential location

It has long been recognized that the spatial structure of urban areas is strongly influenced by transportation costs. In terms of residential location decisions, the dominant factor in transportation cost is usually taken to be the ease and speed of commuting by private automobiles or public transportation. Highway improvements and the development of rapid transit tend to reduce the locational advantage of the central city relative to the suburbs, and result in a lower density, more dispersed residential pattern.[5]

The empirical estimates derived here allow at least tentative prediction of the relative impact of transportation improvements on residential location among income classes. In general, we have seen that lower-income families are more responsive than higher-income families to employment opportunities *within the community*. But with regard to accessibility to employment in *other* communities, the pattern is less clear. Over the middle income ranges, the same pattern of decreasing response with increasing income seems to hold, ceteris paribus. Very low-income households, however—those below $3000—seem to be less responsive than middle-income families to this measure of accessibility, while very high-income households—those above $25,000—are much more responsive. Moreover, changes in accessibility as a result of transportation improve-

---

[5] Muth, for example, argues, "Of all the forces making for urban decentralization during the 1950's, lower marginal transport costs . . . have been by far the most important quantitatively [*Cities and Housing*, p. 324]."

II. Implications for public policy

ments will have an indirect effect on the location of households below the $10,000 income level, through their effects on rents. In general, the tendency of improved accessibility to raise rents will offset 30 to 40 percent of the direct (positive) effect of the accessibility variable on gross residential densities in these income classes. Taking these indirect effects into account, the response to changes in accessibility appears to be smallest in the lowest income class, somewhat higher (and relatively uniform) across the next three income classes, and much higher in the highest income class. This means that further reductions in transportation costs are likely to accentuate the existing economic segregation between the low-income central city and the high-income suburbs.

Tax policies

The empirical analysis provides insights into at least two aspects of property taxation that are of interest to local policymakers: the incidence of the tax and its locational impact.

Property taxation is routinely castigated as being regressive with respect to income. But most of the empirical investigations of tax incidence by income class have been based on the assumption that occupants, whether owners or renters, bear the nonland component of the property tax. If property tax differentials are capitalized, as this investigation indicates, then this regressivity may be substantially eased, since renters tend to be concentrated in the lower income range. If, indeed, property taxation is not regressive, one of the strongest arguments against local governmental reliance upon this source of revenue is eliminated.

It should be emphasized that the regression results with regard to residential rents indicate only that property tax *differentials* are capitalized. It is possible that the portion of the tax on residential property that is common to all municipalities is shifted to tenants. Even so, landlords would still bear a substantial portion of the tax on rental properties; in the sample of communities studied here, equalized tax rates ranged from 1.9 percent to 5.9 percent of market value. Moreover, the highest rate was found in the large, relatively low-income central city. Capitalization of even the differentials in tax burden, then, would relieve low-income renters of a substantial portion of the tax.

The empirical findings with regard to the locational impact of the property tax tend to confirm the fears universally expressed by local administrators. Property tax differentials do exert a significant influence upon the location of at least two types of activity, manufacturing employment and high-income ($10,000–$24,999) residence. In the latter case, however, this effect will be partially, and perhaps wholly, offset if higher tax rates mean higher quality municipal services, particularly in the areas of public education and parks and recreation. Manufacturing, on the other hand, is not sensitive to any of the municipal services included in the model, and municipal governments may therefore expect high tax rates, even when coupled with high quality services, to exert a strong disincentive effect upon this industry. This finding implies that low-tax suburban communities can expect relatively faster growth of tax base than high-tax central-city communities, resulting in a potential for even greater tax rate disparities.

The locational effect of tax rate differentials on manufacturing employment also has implications for the residential distribution of the low-income population. We have already seen that low-income households are much more strongly attracted by employment opportunities within the community than are higher-income households. Thus, to the extent that property tax differentials lead to a decentralization of manufacturing employment, one might expect a concomitant decentralization of the low-income population.

Finally, the locational effects of tax rate differentials may have an indirect effect upon the level of services provided by local governments. If local governments feel constrained to hold down tax rates in order to compete for industry, they may pro-

II. Implications for public policy 117

vide lower quality services than they would otherwise. This effect (which, incidentally, depends less upon the actual existence of locational effects than upon a belief that they exist) may be an important factor in fostering underconsumption of public services at the local level.

Several policies are available to the state and federal governments to reduce property tax differentials and, therefore, the locational effects of such differentials. The most straightforward approach would be some form of unrestricted intergovernmental transfers, or revenue sharing, from the state or federal government to localities, under a formula that provided larger grants to high-tax communities. This would allow a general reduction in property tax rates, along with a narrowing of tax rate differentials. There are a number of ways in which a revenue-sharing formula could be structured to focus aid, more or less specifically, on high-tax communities. The most direct approach would be to include in the formula some measure of tax effort, but less direct methods—such as including a measure of poverty incidence—would also tend to favor high-tax communities.

A second method of providing fiscal relief and reducing tax differentials would be through the assumption by state or federal government of part or all of the cost of specific functions of local government, either through grants-in-aid or direct administration. The single most promising area for this type of fiscal relief is, of course, public education, which accounts for more than 40 percent of spending by local governments from their own revenues; the only other areas where earmarked state or federal aid would seem to be appropriate are public assistance, health and hospitals, and housing, which together account for about 15 percent of local expenditures.[6] Intergovernmental aid for specific functions such as these may, however, be subject to a number of policy objectives that take precedence over

---

[6] U. S. Bureau of the Census, *Governmental Finance in 1968–1969*, Series GF 69, No. 5 (Washington, D. C.: U. S. Government Printing Office, 1970): 22.

elimination of property tax differentials. It may, therefore, be difficult to structure the aid formula so as to further that objective as directly as with general revenue-sharing grants. Moreover, since functional grants are likely to be tied to expenditure levels, existing expenditure patterns may generate an undesirable grant distribution from the standpoint of tax rate equalization. Finally, if the grants are based on a matching formula, they are likely to involve substantial price effects, which may distort the allocation of resources among local functions.

A variation of intergovernmental transfers for specific functions that holds great promise for the equalization of property tax rates is metropolitan finance of local services. True metropolitan consolidation of services, with all property in the metropolitan area taxed at a single rate, would, by definition, eliminate intraurban tax rate differentials. Short of that, there are a variety of forms of metropolitan consolidation that would greatly reduce tax differentials. The recent federal court decision requiring consolidation of central-city and suburban public school systems in Richmond, Virginia, and the California Supreme Court ruling calling for equalization of local tax bases for educational finance within the state may indicate a trend toward one or another of these forms of tax equalization.

It should also be noted that any form of fiscal relief that results in equalization of municipal service levels, particularly in the case of education, will tend to slow the trend toward decentralization of high-income households.

Income maintenance policies

Extension of income maintenance benefits to the working poor may have a significant effect upon the residential location of low-income families. First, by raising the incomes of poverty-level families, such a program may well lessen the high premium these households place upon proximity to employment centers. We have seen that the influence of employment density within the community upon residential location declines

II. Implications for public policy

steadily as income rises. Second, the increase in income will be reflected in an increased demand among low-income families for higher quality housing. Hugh Nourse has estimated that a relatively modest income maintenance program would have induced almost one-quarter of those households living in substandard rental units in 1960 to upgrade their units to standard.[7] The bulk of this increased demand might well be satisfied through renovation of substandard units in the central city. However, it seems reasonable to anticipate that at least some families would seek better housing in suburban communities. The strength of this effect would obviously depend crucially upon the level of support offered by the program. In any case, the high degree of sensitivity of low-income families to residential rents, revealed by the empirical estimates derived here, indicates that policies that increase the housing consumption of the poor have significant potential for affecting residential location.

Labor market policies

Aside from housing costs, the single dominant influence on the location of low-income families appears to be employment opportunities. Policies that affect either the employability of low-income workers or the employment opportunities they face may significantly affect their location decisions.

Possibly the most direct locational effects would result from a program of public employment that creates job opportunities for low-income or unemployed workers. Public employment in central-city areas could be expected to contribute to further centralization of the poor; creation of jobs in the suburbs could be expected to contribute to decentralization.

Less direct effects might flow from vocational training pro-

---

[7] Hugh O. Nourse, "The Effect of a Negative Income Tax on the Number of Substandard Housing Units," *Land Economics* 46(November 1970): 435–446.

grams designed to upgrade skills. Programs that significantly increase earning power might lead to much the same sort of income effects as an income maintenance program. To the extent that training broadens the range of employment for which the worker is suited, it may also widen his options with regard to residential location. Finally, the nature of the employment referral system for graduates of the training program may have an important effect on their residential location.

Concluding remarks

The policy implications drawn here are necessarily qualitative and speculative. The empirical model was not designed to incorporate the entire range of policy variables that may affect urban location decisions. Still, these estimates make clear that there are substantial interactions between those variables that can be affected by public policy—particularly housing costs and accessibility to employment opportunities—and the spatial distribution of households by income class. Moreover, these effects appear to be strongest for poverty-level households.

In designing policies to deal with urban problems, then, public officials at all levels of government would do well to give explicit attention to the potential locational impacts of governmental actions. And students of urban economics should strive to achieve a better integration of local public finance and urban location theory than has existed to date. If this study serves no other purpose, it is hoped that it will demonstrate the importance and feasibility of such an integration.

APPENDIX

Sources of data for cities and towns

1. Department of Civil Engineering, Massachusetts Institute of Technology, Cambridge (Professor A. J. Bone and Mr. Tom Harvey):
   — Average highway travel times, afternoon peak hour (4 P.M. to 5 P.M.) between 111 traffic zones in the Boston area, inside Route 128, in 1963 (unpublished table).
2. Eastern Massachusetts Regional Planning Project, Massachusetts Department of Public Works, 80 Broad Street, Boston:
   — Employment (at place of work) in manufacturing, retail trade, and all other industries, in 1963 (unpublished tables);
   — Acres of land devoted to employment and residence, in 1963 (unpublished tables);
   — Gross acres of developable land (unpublished table);
   — Total developed acres of land, in 1963 (unpublished table);
   — Average highway travel times, afternoon peak hour (4 P.M. to 5 P.M.) between selected points in Boston area outside Route 128, in 1963 (unpublished table).
3. Massachusetts Department of Commerce, *Town and City Monographs:*

- Educational expenditures per pupil in public schools, in 1960–1961 (Section IV. A. 4);
- Minimum zoned residential lot size, in square feet, by class of residence, in 1960 (Section VIII. B.).

4. Massachusetts Department of Commerce, Division of Planning and Research, *Statistics of Massachusetts Cities and Towns by Sub Regions,* September, 1963:
   - Total assessed valuation of land and buildings, in 1960, based on data from the Massachusetts Department of Corporations and Taxation.

5. Massachusetts Federation of Taxpayers Association, *Tax Talk:*
   - Nominal and equalized property tax rates in Massachusetts, based on data provided by the Massachusetts Department of Corporations and Taxation, published annually in the October issue.

6. Metropolitan Area Planning Council, 44 School Street, Boston (Mr. John Culp):
   - Acres of land devoted to ten categories of land use, in 1963 (unpublished tables).

7. New England Insurance Rating Association, 89 Broad Street, Boston:
   - Annual fire insurance premium for $20,000 coverage, single-family brick and frame house, in 1959 (unpublished table);
   - Annual burglary insurance premium for $100,000 coverage, prime risk industrial property, in 1960 (unpublished table).

8. Schroedl, David, *Land as an Investment,* unpublished Master's dissertation, Massachusetts Institute of Technology, Course XV, 1963, Appendix:
   - Average value of taxable land in communities in the Boston area, in 1962, based on assessed values and ratios of market sale values to assessed values provided by the Massachusetts Department of Corporations and Taxation.

9. Town Government Reports (by city or town), Massachusetts State Library, State House, Boston:
   - Expenditures of municipal governments in 1960 by function, for towns with 1960 population under 10,000.

10. U. S. Department of Commerce, Bureau of the Census, *1963 U. S. Census of Business:*
    - Employment (at place of work) in wholesale trade (Vol. V, pp. 23:8–23:10).

11. U. S. Department of Commerce, Bureau of the Census, *1962 U. S. Census of Governments:*

Sources of data for cities and towns 123

- Expenditures of municipal governments in 1960, by function, for cities and towns with 1960 population over 10,000 (Vol. VII, No. 21, Table 33).
12. U. S. Department of Commerce, Bureau of the Census, *1960 U. S. Census of Housing:*
    - Median monthly gross rent of dwelling units and median number of rooms per renter-occupied dwelling unit (Vol. I, Pt. 4, Tables 17, 21, 24, and 27);
    - Number of dilapidated dwelling units, number of dwelling units in deteriorating condition, and total number of dwelling units (Vol. I, Pt. 4, Tables 12, 18, 22, 25, and 27).
13. U. S. Department of Commerce, Bureau of the Census, *1960 U. S. Census of Population:*
    - Number of households by income class, and median family income (Vol. I, Pt. 23, Table 76);
    - Enrollment in public and private primary and secondary schools (Vol. I, Pt. 23, Table 73).

Bibliography

Books and monographs

Alevizos, John P., and Allen E. Beckwith. *Downtown and Suburban Shopping Habits of Greater Boston.* Boston University, College of Business Administration. Boston, Massachusetts: Boston Herald and Traveler, 1964.

Alonso, William. *Location and Land Use: Toward a General Theory of Land Rent.* Cambridge, Massachusetts: Harvard University Press, 1964.

Beck, Morris. *Property Taxation and Urban Land Use: Interaction of Local Taxes and Urban Development in the Northeastern New Jersey Metropolitan Region.* Washington, D. C.: Urban Land Institute, 1963.

Bloom, C. C. *State and Local Tax Differentials.* Iowa City, Iowa: Bureau of Business Research, State University of Iowa, 1955.

Brazer, Harvey Elliot, ed. *Michigan Tax Study: Staff Papers.* Lansing, Michigan, 1958.

Chemical Rubber Company. *Standard Mathematical Tables.* Cleveland, Ohio: Chemical Rubber Co., 1957.
Commonwealth of Pennsylvania, Tax Study Committee. *The Tax Problem.* Philadelphia, Pennsylvania, 1953.
Dunn, Edgar Streeter, Jr. *The Location of Agricultural Production.* Gainesville, Florida: University of Florida Press, 1954.
Floyd, Joe Summers. *Effects of Taxation on Industrial Location.* Chapel Hill, North Carolina: University of North Carolina Press, 1952.
Haber, W., et al. *The Michigan Economy.* Kalamazoo, Michigan: The W. E. Upjohn Institute for Employment Research, 1959.
Hoover, Edgar Malone. *The Location of Economic Activity.* New York: McGraw-Hill, 1948.
Isard, Walter. *Location and Space Economy: A General Theory Relating to Industrial Location, Market Areas, Land Use, Trade, and Urban Structure.* New York: John Wiley and Sons, 1956.
Johnston, John J. *Econometric Methods.* New York: McGraw-Hill, 1963.
Kain, John, John Meyer, and Martin Wohl. *The Urban Transportation Problem.* Cambridge, Massachusetts: Harvard University Press, 1965.
Massachusetts Department of Commerce. *Town and City Monographs.* (Annual) 1960, 1961.
Massachusetts Department of Commerce, Division of Planning and Research. *Statistics of Massachusetts Cities and Towns by Sub Region.* 1963.
Massachusetts Department of Commerce and the Urban and Regional Studies Section, Massachusetts Institute of Technology. *The Effects of Large Lot Size on Residential Development.* Urban Land Institute Technical Institute Bulletin No. 32. Washington, D. C.: Urban Land Institute, 1958.
McGraw-Hill Publishing Company. *Plant Site Survey, A Study Among Business Week Subscribers,* 1964.
Muth, Richard F. *Cities and Housing.* Chicago, Illinois: The University of Chicago Press, 1969.
Netzer, Dick. *Economics of the Property Tax.* Washington, D. C.: The Brookings Institution, 1966.
Olsen, Edgar O. *A Welfare Economic Evaluation of Public Housing,* Ph.D. dissertation, Rice University, 1968.
Report of the Governor's Minnesota Tax Study Committee. St. Paul, Minnesota, 1956.
Seligman, Edwin Robert Anderson. *The Shifting and Incidence of Taxation* (5th edition): New York: Columbia University Press, 1927.

Schroedl, David. *Land as an Investment.* Master's dissertation, Massachusetts Institute of Technology, Course XV, 1963.

Soule, Donald Marion. *Comparative Total Tax Load of Selected Manufacturers.* Lexington, Kentucky: University of Kentucky, 1960.

Strasma, John D. *State and Local Taxation of Industry: Some Comparisons.* Boston, Massachusetts: Federal Reserve Bank of Boston, 1959.

Thompson, Wilbur, and John Mattila. *An Econometric Model of Postwar State Industrial Development.* Detroit, Michigan: Wayne State University Press, 1959.

Turvey, Ralph. *The Economics of Real Property: An Analysis of Property Value and Patterns of Use.* London: George Allen and Unwin, 1957.

U. S. Bureau of the Census. *Current Population Reports,* Series P. 60, No. 81, "Characteristics of Low-Income Population, 1970." Washington, D. C.: U. S. Government Printing Office.

U. S. Bureau of the Census. *Governmental Finance in 1968–1969,* Series GF 69, No. 5. Washington, D. C.: U. S. Government Printing Office, 1970.

U. S. Bureau of the Census. *U. S. Census of Governments, 1962.* Washington, D. C.: U. S. Government Printing Office.

U. S. Bureau of the Census. *U. S. Census of Housing, 1960,* Vol. IV, "Components of Inventory Change," Part 1. Washington, D. C.: U. S. Government Printing Office.

U. S. Bureau of the Census. *U. S. Census of Housing, 1960,* Vol. V, "Residential Finance," Part 1. Washington, D. C.: U. S. Government Printing Office.

U. S. Bureau of the Census. *U. S. Census of Population, 1960,* Vol. I, Part 23. Washington, D. C.: U. S. Government Printing Office.

Wingo, Lowden, Jr. *Transportation and Urban Land.* Washington, D. C.: Resources for the Future, 1961.

Yntema, Dwight Baldwin. *Michigan's Taxes on Business.* Holland, Michigan: Klaasen Printing Co., 1959.

Periodicals and papers

Black, David E. "The Nature and Extent of Effective Property Tax Rate Variation within the City of Boston," *National Tax Journal* 25(June 1972): 203–210.

Campbell, A. K. "Taxes and Industrial Location in the New York

Metropolitan Region," *National Tax Journal* 11(September 1958): 195–218.

Carroll, J. Douglass. "Spatial Interaction and the Urban Metropolitan Regional Description," *Regional Science Association Proceedings*, Vol. I, 1955.

Coen, Robert M., and Brian J. Powell. "Theory and Measurement of the Incidence of Differential Property Tax on Rental Housing," *National Tax Journal* 25(June 1972): 211–216.

Coke, James G., and Charles S. Liebman, "Political Values and Population Density Control," *Land Economics* 37(1961): 347–361.

de Leeuw, Frank, Sam H. Leaman, and Helen Blank. "The Design of a Housing Allowance," Washington, D. C., Urban Institute Working Paper No. 112-25, 1970.

Due, John F. "Studies of State–Local Tax Influences on Location of Industry," *National Tax Journal* 14(June 1961): 163–173.

Ellickson, Bryan. "Jurisdictional Fragmentation and Residential Choice," *Proceedings of the American Economic Association* (May 1971): 334–339.

Haig, Robert M. "Toward an Understanding of the Metropolis," *Quarterly Journal of Economics* 40(1926): 179–208, 402–434.

Hawtrey, Ralph. "Production Functions and Land: A New Approach," *The Economic Journal* 70(March 1960): 114–124.

Heinberg, J. D., and W. E. Oates. "The Incidence of Differential Property Taxes on Urban Housing: A Comment and Some Further Evidence," *National Tax Journal* 23(March 1970): 92–98.

Hoover, Edgar M. "The Evolving Form and Organization of the Metropolis." Paper presented to the Resources for the Future Conference on Urban Economics, Washington, D. C., January 1967.

Ikle, F. C. "Sociological Relationship of Traffic to Population and Distance," *Traffic Quarterly* (April 1954).

Kain, John F. "Journey-to-Work as a Determinant of Residential Location," *Regional Science Association Proceedings* 9(1962): 137–160.

Lowry, Ira S. "Location Parameters in the Pittsburgh Model," *Regional Science Association Proceedings* 11(1963): 145–165.

Margolis, Julius. "On Municipal Land Policy for Fiscal Gains," *National Tax Journal* 9(September 1956): 247–257.

Margolis, Julius. "Municipal Fiscal Structure in a Metropolitan Region," *Journal of Political Economy* 65(June 1957): 225–236.

McGraw-Hill Publishing Company. "Plant Site Preferences of Industry and Factors of Selection," *Business Week Research Report*, 1958.

McMillan, T. E. "Determinants of Plant Location," *Land Economics* 41(August 1965): 239–246.

Mills, Edwin S. "An Aggregative Model of Resource Allocation in a Metropolitan Area," *Proceedings of the American Economic Association* (May 1967): 197–210.

Nourse, Hugh O. "The Effect of a Negative Income Tax on the Number of Substandard Housing Units," *Land Economics* 46(November 1970): 435–446.

Oldman, Oliver, and Henry Aaron. "Assessment-Sales Ratios under the Boston Property Tax," *National Tax Journal* 18(March 1965): 36–49.

Orr, Larry L. "The Incidence of Differential Property Taxes on Urban Housing," *National Tax Journal* 21(September 1968): 253–262.

Ross, W. D. "Tax Concessions and Their Effect," *Proceedings of the National Tax Association* (1957): 216–224.

Smolensky, Eugene. "Public Housing or Income Supplements: The Economics of Housing for the Poor," *Journal of the American Institute of Planners* 34(March 1968): 94–101.

Stegman, Michael A. "Comment on 'Public Housing or Income Supplements: The Economics of Housing for the Poor,'" *Journal of the American Institute of Planners* 34(May 1968): 195–198.

Tiebout, Charles M. "A Pure Theory of Local Expenditures," *Journal of Political Economy* 64(October 1956): 416–424.

Townsend, Roswell G. "Inequalities of Residential Property Taxation in Metropolitan Boston," *National Tax Journal* 4(December 1951): 361–369.

Woodard, F. O., and Ronald W. Brady. "Inductive Evidence of Tax Capitalization," *National Tax Journal* 18(June 1965): 193–201.

Index

A

Accessibility
  to economic activities
    influence of, on quality index, 44
    in models, 13
  effect of
    on manufacturing and wholesale employment gross density, 96
    on manufacturing employment gross density, 95
    on median gross rent per room, 86
    on professional and governmental employment gross density, 94-95
    on retail employment gross density, 90
  elasticities with respect to, 73-74
  to employment, 72-74
    estimated elasticities with respect to, 70
  as generalized accessibility variable, 47
  by income class, 5, 104
  in location decisions, 46-47
  measures of, in quality index, 41
  to product and factor markets, in urban location theory, 45
  variables, 45-47
Administration of municipal services by state or federal governments, 117
Alevizos, John P., 93n.
Alonso, William, 11, 12n., 38, 67n., 72, 73n.
Alonso model, 67, 72-73
Areal share
  affected by land value, 68
  determined by competitive bidding, 31, 32
  of developed land in model, 17

131

effect of density zoning on, 39
minimum lot size elasticity of, 76
relation to gross density, 34

B

Beck, Morris, 58n.
Beckwith, Allen E., 93
Blank, Helen, 111n.
Bloom, C. C., 9n.
Boston dummy variable
  effect of
    on manufacturing and wholesale employment gross density, 96
    on manufacturing employment gross density, 95
    on professional and governmental employment gross density, 93-94
    on retail employment gross density, 90-92
Boston SMSA, 56n.
Boston urbanized area
  median family income of, 60-61
  population of, 61
  sample region, 59-63
Burglary insurance, estimated elasticities with respect to, 71, see also Police and fire protection
Burglary and fire insurance premiums
  effect of, on median gross rent per room, 86

C

Capital input prices in model, 19
Carroll, J. Douglas, 46n.
Central city
  poor affected by lower quality municipal services in, 4
  poor in, 2
Centralization of poor by public employment programs, 119
Chemical Rubber Company, 65n.
Code enforcement, effects of, on location of low-income residential use, 110
Coke, James G., 11n.

Competitive bidding
  sites allocated by, 31-32
Complementary land uses, gross density of, 34
Condition of housing, see Housing

D

Decentralization of poor
  effect of density zoning on, 113-114
  effect of urban renewal and code enforcement on, 112
de Leeuw, Frank, 111n.
Density zoning
  discrimination against land uses by, 35
  effect of, 37
    on areal shares, 113
    on decentralization of poor, 113-114
    on low density residential patterns, 3
    on low-income residential uses, 75
    on net residential density, 53, 106, 113
    on occupancy, 74
    on urban land use, 113
  in *Hypothesis 3*, 5, 105-106
  interference in free market, 77
  in model, 8
  regulations
    exclude poor from suburbs, 5, 105-106
    in model, 21
  studies of, 11
Dilapidated and deteriorating housing, effect of, on residential location, 79-80
Distance exponent, 46n.
Due, John F., 9n.

E

Education
  expenditures on
    capitalization of, 86-87
    effect of
      on median gross rent per room, 86, 87

Index

on residential land uses, 82-84
relation to fiscal relief, 117
in location decisions of high-income
    families, 105
quality of
    poor in central city affected by lower,
        4
    measures of, 47-48
Educational expenditures per pupil
    estimated elasticities with respect to, 71
    stability in sample of, tested, 63
Ellickson, Bryan, 10n., 12n.
Employment density
    estimated elasticities of, 70, 73-74
Employment density, gross
    effect of
        on land values, 99-101
        on median gross rent per room, 86
    as measure of accessibility to employ-
        ment opportunities, 42
    as measure of employment opportun-
        ities, 46
    in net residential density equation, 66
Employment density, net, in tests of
    model, 64-67, 68
Employment opportunities
    distribution of, affected by land and
        property tax costs, 5
    effect of
        on residential location, 45
        on low-income residential use, 3, 5,
            119
    effect on residential land use, 72-74
    in *Hypothesis 4*, 5, 103, 106-107
    in *Hypothesis 1*, 5, 103, 105
    increase value of residential land, 32
    industrial and residential location
        linked in model by, 116
    interrelated with residential location
        and municipal services, 4
    measure of, 46
    for poor diminished in central city, 4
Equilibrium locus, 25-26
External diseconomies created by indus-

tries, effect of, on proximity to
    employment opportunities, 86

F

Fire and burglary insurance premiums,
    effect on median gross rent per
    room, 86
Fire and police protection, *see* Police and
    fire protection
Fire insurance
    estimated elasticities with respect to, 71
    premiums, 85

G

Grants-in-aid, 117
    property tax differentials reduced by,
        117
Gross density
    definition, 40
    determination of, interpreting results
        for, 29
    effect of minimum lot size zoning on,
        39
    equations explaining, for eight land
        uses, 42
    of high-income residence, *see* High-
        income residential uses
    land use, average price of land as linear
        function of, 44
    in model, 17
    obtained by substituting net density
        and areal share, 34
    variables defined for eight land uses,
        41
Gross revenue function, 23

H

Hawtrey, Sir Ralph, 30n.
Health and hospitals, unsuitable in model,
    52
High-income residential uses
    capital-land input ratio for, 38-39
    in *Hypothesis 2*, 5, 104-105

land value as measure of site costs for, 43
net effect of minimum lot size zoning on gross density for, 39
Highways, *see* Streets and highways
Highway travel time in index of accessibility to economic activity, 45-46
Hoover, Edgar Malone, 97
Household density, *see* Residential density
Housing
  allowances, effects of, on low-income residential uses, 111-113
  condition index
    estimated elasticities with respect to, 71
    in model, 52-53
  conditions
    effect of
      on median gross rent per room, 86, 88-89
      on rents, 89
      on residential land uses, 79-80
    measures of, in quality index, 41
  costs
    effect of, on low-income residential uses, 5
    in *Hypothesis 1*, 5, 103-104
    by income class, 5, 104
  demand for
    effect of, on capitalization of municipal service benefits, 88
    effect of elastic, on capitalization of property tax differentials, 88, 108
    in property tax shifting, 56
    market in model, 20
  policies and low-income residential uses, 109-114
  programs, *see also* Housing allowances; Housing vouchers; Rent certificates; Rent supplements
    effect of, on low-income residential uses, 111-113
  services output in model, 19
  stock as input into production of housing services, 16
  supply
    effect on capitalization of property tax differentials of inelastic, 108
    effect on capitalization of municipal service benefits and property tax differential of, 88
  vouchers, effects on low-income residential uses of, 111-113
Hypotheses to be tested, 5, 103-108

I

Ikle, F. C., 46n.
Income maintenance policies, effect of, on low-income residential uses, 118-119
Industrial enclave, services and property tax rate in, 57-58
Intercommunity differentials, tests of stability of, 63
Intergovernmental transfers, unrestricted, 117-118
Interurban location decisions, studies of, 9
Intraurban location decisions
  effect of property tax on, 9
  studies of, 9

J

Johnston, John J., 62n.

K

Kain, John F., 73

L

Labor
  input prices in model, 19
  market policy
    public employment as, affects low-income residential uses, 119
    vocational training as, affects low-

Index

income residential uses, 119-120
Land costs, *see also* Land values; Land rents
   affect employment opportunities, 5
   in *Hypothesis 4*, 5, 106-107
   in manufacturing and wholesale employment, 107
Land market
   model, Ricardian, 7
   space allocated by urban, 7
Land rent
   in absence of lot size zoning, 35-37
   in configuration 1, 37
   in configuration 2, 38
   determined endogenously, 30
   as function of net density and site quality, 24
   gross density functions linear in, 34
   high density allows low, 3
   interpreted as gross land rent, 29
   and land density in model, 27
   land value in model determining, 39
   as measure of land user's annual costs, 73
   in model, 7, 23
   testing relationships among land use densities, site characteristics, and, 41
Land use
   categories, 41-43
   density affected by distance from core, 13
   nonresidential, employment as a measure of, 42
   nonresidential classification, 42
   residential, divided by income level, 42
Land uses
   complementarity among, 32
Land value
   determinants of, 98-101
      employment densities, 99-101
      gross household densities, 99-101
      median family income, 99-101
   determination of, 7
   effect of
      on manufacturing and wholesale employment gross density, 96-97
      on manufacturing employment gross density, 95-97
      on median gross rent per room, 86, 87
      on professional and governmental employment gross density, 94-95
      on residential land uses, 81-82
      on retail employment gross density, 90, 92
   estimated elasticities with respect to average, 71
   excluded from gross density regression, 82n.-83n.
   expression for market, 39-40
   measure of, 43
   as measure of competing bids for land, 78
   as measure of competing bids from other land uses, 69
   as measure of site costs, 43
   problems in quantifying, 109
   property tax defined in terms of, 28
   in test of model, 64-65
Leaman, Sam H., 111n.
Liebman, Charles S., 11n.
Low-income
   residential location and housing policies, 109-114
   residential use
      capital-land input ratio for, 38-39
      correlated with substandard housing index, 53
      discriminated against by density zoning, 35
      effect of density zoning on, 53, 75
      effect of minimum lot size zoning on gross density for, 39
      in *Hypothesis 1*, 5, 103-104
      rent variable as measure for, 43
Lowry, Ira S., 73

M

McMillan, T. E., 10n.
Manufacturing and wholesale employment gross density, determinants of, 96-98
  accessibility index, 96
  Boston dummy variable, 96
  gross household density, 96
  land values, 96-97
  property tax rate, 96-98
  provision of water and sewerage services, 96
  retail employment gross density, 96-97
Manufacturing classified as nonresidential land use, 42
Manufacturing employment gross density, determinants of, 95-98
  accessibility index, 95
  Boston dummy variable, 95
  gross household density, 95
  land values, 95-97
  property tax rate, 95-98
  provision of water and sewerage services, 95
  retail employment gross density, 95
Massachusetts
  Department of Corporations and Taxation, 60n.
  Department of Public Works, 60n., 89
  Federation of Taxpayers Association, 60n.
Mattila, John, 9n.
Median family income
  effect of
    on land values, 99-101
    on median gross rent per room, 86
    on professional and governmental employment gross density, 94-95
    on residential rent regression, 86
    on retail employment gross density, 90, 92-93
  in sample communities, 61
Median gross rent per room
  determinants of
    accessibility, 86, 88
    burglary and fire insurance premiums, 86
    educational expenditures per pupil, 86-87
    expenditures on highways, 86
    expenditures on parks and recreation, 86
    gross employment density, 86
    housing conditions, 86, 88-89
    land values, 86, 87
    median family income, 86
    provision of water and sewerage services, 86, 87
  effect of, on residential land uses, 77-79
  estimated elasticities of, 70
  as measure of residential rental value, 43
  in regression, 69
  and substandard housing index, 53
Mills, Edwin S., 12n.
Minimum zoned lot size, 53-54, *see also* Density zoning
  effect of, on residential land uses, 74-77
  in equation, 66
  estimated elasticities with respect to, 70
Model, preliminary tests of, 64
Mortgage guarantees influence on urban location decisions, 109
Municipal service benefits, capitalization of, 87-88
Municipal services, *see also* Education; Parks and recreation; Police and fire protection; Streets and highways; Water, sewerage, and sanitation services
  services
    capitalized into rents and property value, 57
    difficulties in quantifying, 109
    difficulty of financing central city, 3
    excluded from empirical analysis, 51
    as exogenously determined site characteristics, 34
    finance variables affect high-income residential location, 5
    financing in *Hypothesis 2*, 5, 104-105

Index

interrelated with residential location and employment opportunities, 4
metropolitan financing of, 118
in model, 8
quality of
  difficulties in specifying, 42
  lower, in central city where affects poor, 4
  measures in quality index, 41
  in quality index, 44, 47-53
state or federal administration of, 117
tax revenues provide, 56
Muth, Richard F., 12n., 109n., 114n.

N

Net density
  in absence of lot size zoning, 35-37
  affects land rent, 24
  effect of minimum zoned lot size on, 74
  effect of proportional property tax on equilibrium, 28
  expression used to obtain gross density, 34
  increasing when land prices increase, 29-30
  and land rent in model, 27, 64-68
  minimum lot size elasticity of, 76
  optimal, 29
  and quality index in model, 64-68
  as ratio of nonland to land inputs, 23
  relation to gross density, 17
  in tests, 65-67, 68
Netzer, Dick, 8n., 9n., 108
Nourse, Hugh O., 119

O

Olsen, Edgar O., 111n.
Orr, Larry L., 55n.

P

Parks and recreation
  expenditures for
    effect of
      on median gross rent per room, 86
      on residential land uses, 82-84
  estimated elasticities with respect to, 70
  in *Hypothesis 2*, 104-105
  measures of value of, 51
Police and fire protection
  expenditures for, effect of, on residential land uses, 84-86
  quality of, 49-50
  in residential density equations, 105
Population of sample communities, 61
Potential index, 45-46
Price of land, *see* Land value
Production function in model, 19-20, 22
Professional and governmental employment gross density, determinants of, 93-95
  accessibility, 94-95
  Boston dummy variable, 93-94
  gross residential density, 94-95
  highway expenditures, 94-95
  median family income, 94-95
  price of land, 94-95
  property tax rates, 94-95
Professional and governmental services included in nonresidential land use, 42
Property tax
  affects employment opportunities, 5
  base, relation to tax rate and service expenditures, 57-58
  effect of
    on employment opportunities, 106
    on high-income residential uses, 5
    on manufacturing and wholesale employment gross density, 96-98, 107
    on manufacturing employment gross density, 95-98
    on professional and governmental employment gross densities, 94-95
    on residential land uses, 80-81
    on retail employment gross density, 90, 92

effect of introducing into model, 29
equalized
　estimated elasticities with respect to, 71
　introduced to measure effects of property tax, 54
　in model, 8
　test of stability in sample, 63
excluded from gross density regression, 82n.-83n.
exogenously determined, 81
as exogenously determined site characteristic, 34
growth of, base in low tax communities, 116
homeowner's preferential treatment re, 109
in *Hypothesis 4*, 5, 106-107
in *Hypothesis 2*, 5, 104-105
liabilities capitalized into housing values, 57-58
locational effect of, 56-58, 116
as main source of local tax revenue, 8
measures introduced, 41
measures of the effect of, 54-58
in model, 28
policies, 115-118
problems in quantifying, 109
regulations in model, 21
rising in central city, 4
shifting
　contraction of housing stock effects, 55-56
　on rental housing, 5, 107-108
smaller residential, base in central city, 3
Property tax differentials
affects decentralization of poor, 116
capitalization of, 115
effect of, on gross density of rental housing, 55
means to reduce, 117-118
provision of municipal services affect locational effect of, 116
shifting of, 80, 87
in *Hypothesis 5*, 5, 107-108

Public employment, effect of, on low-income residential uses, 119
Public housing, effect of, on low-income residential uses, 109-111
Public services, *see also* Municipal services
deteriorating, in central city, 4
studies of locational effects of local, 10
Public utilities in analysis, 51-52
Public welfare, unsuitable in model, 52
Pupil-teacher ratio
as explanatory variable, 82
tested for stability in sample, 63

Q

Quality characteristics, 44-53
Quality index
community characteristics assumed to determine, 44
dependent on mix of land uses, 32
in model, 20-21, 27
specified, 41
Quality of land, 25, 26

R

Renovation of substandard units, 89, 113
effect of income maintenance policies on, 118-119
returns to, 88-89, 113
Rental housing
in *Hypothesis 5*, 5, 107-108
as proportion of all housing in Boston SMSA, 43n.-44n.
Rent bids, net rents used as, 31n.
Rent certificates, effect of, on low-income residential uses, 111-113
Rent function
in analysis of density zoning, 35-39
effect of proportional property tax on, 28
in model, 24-28
Rent levels, *see* Residential rents
Rent supplements, effect of, on low-income residential uses, 109, 111-113

Index

Residential density, gross
  affects land values, 99-101
  determinants of
    employment opportunities, 72-74
    expenditures for police and fire protection, water and sewerage services, and highways, 84-86
    expenditures on education and on parks and recreation, 82-84
    housing conditions, 79-80
    land values, 81-82
    median gross rent per room, 77-79
    minimum zoned lot size, 74-77
    property tax rates, 80-81
  effect of
    on manufacturing and wholesale employment gross density, 96
    on manufacturing employment gross density, 95-97
    on professional and governmental employment gross density, 94
    on retail employment gross density, 90, 91
  effect of employment opportunities on, 72-74
  effect of housing index on, 80
  effect of minimum lot zoning on, 74
  effect of residential rents on, 78
  estimated elasticities of, 75
  income classes of, 69
  as proxy for accessibility to labor and product markets, 42
  results of, regressions compared to model, 67
Residential density, net
  as function of site characteristics, 68
  in *Hypothesis 1*, 5, 104
  minimum lot size elasticity of, 76
  in tests of model, 64-67, 68
Residential land uses
  influenced by site characteristics, 68
  and retail trade, 32
Residential location
  of high-income households, *see* High-income residential uses
  interrelated with employment opportunity and municipal services, 4
  of low-income households, *see* Low-income residential uses
Residential property, owner occupied, property tax in gross density regressions for, 54
Residential property, renter occupied, in gross density regression, 54-55
Residential rents
  determinants of, 86
  effect of housing index on, 80
  effect of property tax on, 54-55
  and elasticity of gross density, 78
  as measure of competing bids, 69
Retail employment gross density
  determinants of, 90-93
    accessibility index, 90
    Boston dummy variable, 90-92
    expenditure on highways, 90-91
    median family income, 90, 92-93
    price of land, 90, 92
    property tax, 90, 92
    residential density, 90, 91
  effect on manufacturing and wholesale employment gross density, 96-97
Retail trade
  accessibility index as measure of accessibility to, 46
  as nonresidential classification of land use, 42
  and residential land uses, 32
Revenue function, slope of, 29
  equals price of bundle of nonland inputs in equilibrium, 26
Revenue sharing, *see* Intergovernmental transfers, unrestricted
Revenue sharing grants, problems with, 118
Ross, W. D., 9n.

S

Site characteristics influencing residential land use, 70
Site costs, 43-44

Site rent, *see* Land rent
Smolensky, Eugene, 89, 111n.
Stegman, Michael A., 89
Streets and highways, *see also* Highway travel time
  expenditures on
    effect of
      on median gross rent per room, 86
      on professional and governmental employment gross density, 94-95
      on residential land uses, 84-86
      on retail employment gross density, 90, 91
    estimated elasticities with respect to, 71
  quality of, 48-49
  in residential density equations, 105
Substandard units, 52
Suburb, bedroom, services and tax rates in, 58
Suburbs
  commercial and industrial activity attracted by lower property taxes of, 4
  low-density residential pattern in, 3

T

Tax costs, *see* Property tax
Tax rate, *see* Property tax
Tax rate differentials, *see* Property tax differentials
Thompson, Wilbur, 9n.
Tiebout, Charles M., 10
Transportation policies and residential location, 114-115

U

United States Bureau of Census, 44n., 56, 60n., 117n.

United States Census of Housing, 52
United States Census of Population, 1960, 59n., 61
Urban location theory, previous studies of, 12
Urban renewal
  effect of, on poor, 4
  influence of, on urban location decisions, 109-110
  unsuitable in model, 52

V

Vocational training affects residential location of poor, 119-120

W

Water and sewerage services
  estimated elasticities of lack of municipal, 71
  excluded from gross density regression, 82n.-83n.
  expenditures for
    capitalization of, 87-88
    effect of, on residential land uses, 84-86
  provision of
    effect of
      on manufacturing and wholesale employment gross density, 96
      on manufacturing employment gross density, 95
      on median gross rent per room, 86-87
  in residential density equations, 105
  and sanitation services, quality of, 50-51
Wingo, Lowden, Jr., 12n

Z

Zoning, *see* Density zoning

```
A 4
B 5
C 6
D 7
E 8
F 9
G 0
H 1
I 2
J 3
```